Understanding Culture

Understanding Culture

An Introduction to Anthropological Theory

Philip Carl Salzman
McGill University

WAVELAND

PRESS, INC.

Prospect Heights, Illinois

For information about this book, contact:
    Waveland Press, Inc.
    P.O. Box 400
    Prospect Heights, Illinois 60070
    (847) 634-0081
    www.waveland.com

Contents

Acknowledgments

While writing is often a solitary activity, it is in truth never an individual activity. Always hovering in the writer's brain are the thinkers and writers and teachers, preceding and contemporary, direct and indirect, from whom the writer learned the foundations of what he or she knows. And even more immediate are the colleagues who have shared ideas, argued positions, and challenged accepted ideas, and by so doing have stimulated the writer and the writing. Special thanks must go to those who have generously given direct commentary on the drafts of the manuscript. Making all of this possible is the institutional support of colleagues who have provided the author with funding and free time to bring the work to fruition.

Specifically, I want to thank my colleagues in the Department of Anthropology at McGill University for the course release that gave me time to write this book. Three more distant colleagues provided Waveland with careful and thoughtful anonymous readers' reports on my manuscript. Close by, my excellent colleagues Laurel Bossen, Lisa Marlene Edelsward (with whom I also share a family), John G. Galaty, and Toby Morantz, and from greater distance William Irons, generously sacrificed their valuable time and energy and applied their expertise to examine the manuscript in detail and to offer many astute and helpful comments. To the extent that I have not been able to make the most of these valuable suggestions, the shortcomings of this work remain my responsibility.

I dedicate this book to my colleagues near and far.

Chapter One

Introduction to Theory

> As the dawn begins to fall among the soft brown roofs and the slender
> palm trees stand out against a colourless, gleaming sea, lovers slip
> home from trysts beneath the palm trees or in the shadow of beached
> canoes, that the light may find each sleeper in his appointed place.

So Margaret Mead ([1928] 1973:14) describes the beginning of the day in
Samoa, a group of islands in the fabled South Seas of Polynesia. Mead,
a famous pioneer of American cultural anthropology, went to Samoa in
1926, when she at twenty-three years old and modern anthropology
were both quite young.

Mead went to Samoa to study Samoan culture by means of **ethnographic field research** (see "Glossary" for all terms in bold print),
or, as it is often described, participant-observation. This involves living
for a good period among the people; observing their economic, political,
and ritual activities; and speaking with them to learn their perspectives, attitudes, and values. Mead lived amongst the Samoans for six
months, and then returned to the United States to write her ethnographic report, published in 1928 as *Coming of Age in Samoa*. This
groundbreaking anthropological work became popular and was read by
generations of Americans, not least for its portrayal of free sexuality
among teenagers amidst the palm trees.

Let us consider for a moment how Margaret Mead went about her
research. Not what she saw—for this you can have the pleasure of reading *Coming of Age*—but rather the way in which Mead saw Samoa, its
people, and their culture. Mead did not come to Samoa with an empty
mind like a blank slate or a blank monitor screen, which she would fill
with unselected description based upon undirected observation.
Rather, Mead came to her Samoan research with a theoretical agenda.
That is, her research was guided by **theory**, which we can define min-
imally as a general idea that can be applied to many specific instances
or particular cases.

1

The theory that guided Mead was provided by her research supervisor, Franz Boas, the founder of American anthropology. Boas, by origin a German Jewish geographer, was convinced that differences in human behavior from one place to another were due, not to biological differences of race, but to differences in culture and circumstance: as Boas (foreword in Mead [1928] 1973) puts it, "much of what we ascribe to human nature is no more than a reaction to the restraints put upon us by our civilization." Boas was thus an early advocate of the "nurture" side of what has come to be called the "nature-nurture" debate about the relative influence on human beings of biology versus culture, and he was—not incidentally—a strong opponent of racism. As Mead ("Preface to the 1973 Edition") stated the theoretical position,

> I wrote [Coming of Age in Samoa] as a contribution to our knowledge of how human capacities and human well-being of young people depend on what they learn and on the social arrangements of the society within which they are born and raised.

Noting that Mead had a theoretical agenda in pursuing her research in Samoa is not suggesting that she should have or could have proceeded in any other fashion. Mead, like all researchers, depended upon her theory, and the concepts and categories used in the theory, to guide her observations and inform her conclusions. This is not to say that the theory one holds always and entirely determines **perceptions**, what one sees and learns. But our ideas, what we think, our **cognition**, and our intellectual framework does to a significant degree guide and influence our perceptions. This is true whether or not our theoretical framework is explicit or implicit, systematic or ragtag. However, what we see turns back and influences what we think, at least to a degree. In sum, what we think, our concepts, categories, and ideas, and what we see in the world interact with one another and mutually influence one another. This is one reason why theory, our intellectual framework, is so important in research.

The theory of Boas and Mead, that cultural rather than biological factors determine most differences between human populations, is both very general and not very precise, covering a vast number of cultural and biological facts and a wide range of human differences, but not stating exactly the results expected. A theory this general and imprecise I would call a **heuristic theory**, which serves to direct attention to certain factors, thus setting the research agenda and raising certain expectations about likely research findings. Heuristic theories, because they are so general and imprecise, cannot themselves be proven or refuted, but rather remain influential as long as they are regarded as fruitful in inspiring successful research, as consistent with developing intellectual trends, and as relevant to social and practical concerns.

In order to carry out research on the nature-nurture debate, Mead had to switch from her original interest in social and cultural change in Samoa (which she describes in appendix 3 of *Coming of Age*), to study traditional Samoan culture. She focuses on the development of girls and young women, with special attention to puberty: "[w]hat we wish to test is no less than the effect of civilisation upon a developing human being at the age of puberty" ([1928] 1973:6). Mead ([1928] 1973:2–3) was familiar with the theory of puberty and adolescence widespread in her own culture:

> Adolescence was characterized as the period in which idealism flow-ered and rebellion against authority waxed strong, a period during which difficulties and conflicts were absolutely inevitable. . . . The physical changes [i.e., puberty] which are going on in the bodies of your boys and girls have their definite psychological accompaniments. You can no more evade one than you can the other; as your daughter's body changes from the body of a child to the body of a woman, so inevitably will her spirit change, and that stormily.

This theory, emphasizing the biological basis of human behavior, was held by specialists, such as psychologists, and by the population at large. It was thus both an **academic theory** and a **folk theory** that was part of the culture of North American society.

This biological theory of adolescence, however, contradicts the general, heuristic theory held by Boas and Mead that stressed the influence of culture in understanding and explaining human behavior.

> And on the basis of [the anthropologist's] knowledge of the deter-minism of culture, of the plasticity of human being, he doubted [the biological theory of adolescence]. Were these difficulties due to be-ing adolescent or to being adolescent in America? (Mead [1928] 1973:5)

Mead argues, on the basis of her field research, that Samoan girls as they pass through puberty do not experience the emotional upheaval and social disruption that is called adolescence in America. Samoan girls, according to Mead, experience the period during and after puberty as one of relaxation, lack of stress, enjoyment, and pleasure. Mead explains this in terms of Samoan culture and the traditional life-course of a Samoan teenager. Among the important factors are these: Samoans are part of broad networks of kinship and large households as children, teenagers, and adults. There is thus in Samoa a continuity of family membership rather than, as in America, a break with a "family of orientation" and the construction of a new and separate "family of procreation." Similarly, in traditional Samoa the course of life was clearly laid out, and for the teenager there were few choices and thus few worries about occupation, identity, religion, or politics. In tradi-tional Samoa, a calm and accepting attitude was encouraged, and

intense emotions discouraged, unlike the emotional intensity culti-
vated in American culture. In Samoa, unlike America, sexuality was
gradual, sexual play beginning among young boys and girls, and
casual, not attached to intense emotions or strongly moralized. Thus
for Samoan teenagers, experiencing sexuality at puberty was not a
major break, as in America, but a point in a smooth, gradual transition.
Comparing puberty in Samoa and America, Mead ([1928] 1973:ch. 13)
was able to draw a theoretical conclusion that adolescence, defined as
emotional upheaval and social disruption, accompanied the biological
changes of puberty in some cultures but not in others. More specifically,
cultures such as Samoa characterized by social continuity, a predeter-
mined life course, and emotional placidity would manifest no adolescent angst and rebellion during puberty, whereas cultures such as
America, with sharp breaks in family and social ties, many choices in
occupation, affiliations, and values, and an encouragement of emotional intensity, would be characterized by a strong adolescence with
widespread emotionality and conflict.

Mead's conclusion and theory contradicted the American folk and
psychological theory that adolescence was an inevitable consequence of
biological changes during puberty. Mead believed that her research in
Samoa strongly supported her theory of the cultural determination of
adolescence and refuted the claim that adolescence, like puberty, is universal and exhibited in all human populations. Both the biologically
oriented American folk and psychological theory and Mead's theory of
cultural determination of adolescence, although contradictory in content, can both be considered **substantive theories** (as distinct from
heuristic theories), because they are specific and precise enough to test
through the examination of evidence. This is what Mead did by comparing puberty in two different cultures. According to the biological theory,
adolescence would be the same in both. Mead found that adolescence in
the sense of upheaval and disruption did not exist in Samoa. This finding thus supported her cultural theory and contradicted the biological
theory. The more specific and precise substantive theories thus act as a
link between general heuristic theories, such as that culture or biology
is determining, on the one hand, and specific factual information, for
example the social and psychological patterns found in Samoa or other
ethnographic cases, on the other hand. This connection between the
general idea of a heuristic theory and factual ethnographic material,
via the more specific substantive theory, allows a judgment, based upon
factual evidence, to be made about heuristic theories too general to be
evaluated directly.

Mead's Samoan ethnography **supported** her substantive theory
that a disturbed adolescence results from specific cultural conditions
such as social discontinuity and uncertainty, and thus supported her
heuristic theory that culture is a major determinant of human behav-

ior. But we cannot say that any theory is definitely **proven**, because further information might be inconsistent with the theory. All we can say is that a theory is supported by a great deal of information, and that facts inconsistent with the theory have not so far appeared.

If, as already mentioned, our cognition, what we think, interacts with our perception, what we see, hear, smell, and feel, then **facts** have to be understood as particular bits of information that we learn, rather than as existing independently in the world. In other words, facts are **interpretations** that we make of specific things in the world, interpretations that are based partly on the concepts, categories, and theories that we bring to those specific things. Collecting facts is thus not like collecting stones, which keep their own shape; we shape the facts as we interpret the specific things about which we are doing research. This is one of the reasons that we sometimes get the facts wrong. Any **descriptive account** of the facts, such as the nature of society and puberty in Samoa, is in reality an interpretation. There can therefore be different descriptions of the same situation. Some descriptive accounts may be better than others, in that they provide more and/or more precise evidence. But all descriptive accounts of the facts are as open to debate as are theories.

That the nature of facts is debatable is brought home quite clearly in the case of Mead's *Coming of Age in Samoa*, for her ethnographic description of Samoa has come under vigorous and sustained attack. Derek Freeman, who came to Samoa after Mead but carried out research there for many years, published his critique in *Margaret Mead and Samoa: The Making and Unmaking of an Anthropological Myth* (1983). He argues that because Mead did not know the Samoan language well enough, spent so little time in Samoa, gave her attention mainly to girls, did not apply a rigorous enough methodology, did not give adequate attention to the historical literature on Samoa, and was biased due to her commitment to Boas's theory of cultural determinism, she misinterpreted what she saw and misrepresented Samoan society. Freeman says that careful and full examination of all of the evidence shows that Samoan society was violent rather than placid, competitive rather than inclusive, and restrictive rather than permissive in sexuality. Furthermore, he points out that Mead's ([1928] 1973:ch. 11) cases of deviant girls in her small sample reflects an extremely high level of deviancy, indicating precisely a great deal of emotional upheaval and social disruption at and after puberty!

Freeman concludes that adolescent upheaval was not absent in Samoa, and therefore, contra-Mead, the Samoan case was not a refutation of the biological theory that puberty results in a stormy adolescence. Freeman thus argues that the Samoan case does not provide support for Mead's substantive theory of the cultural determination of adolescence or Boas's heuristic theory of the cultural determination of human behavior. Freeman himself takes the heuristic position that biology and culture are both major determinants and often interact with one another in human life and development. However, the issue did not end with Freeman, for many other researchers were led to reexamine Mead's work and Freeman's critique and the broader literature on Samoa; this new research has brought to light new and important evidence. Some researchers (e.g., Grant 1995; Shankman 1996) have argued that close examination of the evidence supports Mead's interpretation, while others maintain that Freeman is correct. The debate continues.

This anthropological examination of coming of age in Samoa illustrates the many parts that theory plays in research about human life. Let us review what we have seen. First, each abstract and general heuristic theory provides a broad idea about the world and human beings. Heuristic theory, pointing to what is important and significant, sets an agenda for thinking about the world and for carrying out research. Heuristic theory is so abstract and imprecise that it is impossible to bring factual evidence directly to bear on it. Second, in order to conduct research, a more limited and specific theoretical formulation is needed. This substantive theory addresses a specific topic, such as adolescence, specifying the relationships between features, such as between culture, puberty, and adolescence. Substantive theory must be formulated in such a way that factual description would support it or refute it. Third, however much **evidence**, factual description of observable particulars such as specific behaviors, is brought to bear, a theory can never be proven absolutely but at best can be strongly supported by a large amount of evidence and all of the evidence. Fourth, the descriptive facts that are cited as evidence for or against a theory do not exist independently in nature, but are interpretations, constructed by individual researchers and others by applying their own thinking processes, cognition, to the activity of observation, and thus influencing their perception. This means that facts can be contested, challenged, and debated, as in the Mead-Freeman debate, and that further scrutiny can lead to reinterpretation of the facts. Fifth and finally, both theories and facts are needed, for theories without facts are void of substance, and facts without theories are insignificant.

META-THEORY

The heuristic and substantive theories of Boas and Mead and of the American psychologists that we have discussed are based upon certain **assumptions** about knowledge, how we gain knowledge, what knowledge is worthwhile, and how we know when we know something. These assumptions about knowledge are **philosophical** assumptions;

more specifically, philosophical inquiries and theories about knowledge are called **epistemology**, the study of knowledge. These philosophical inquiries, which are logically prior to heuristic and substantive theory, are called **meta-theory**. Heuristic and substantive theories are about the world; meta-theory is about knowledge and the construction of theories about the world.

The **epistemological theory** held by Boas and Mead and the American psychologists was widely held and is familiar to all readers of this book; the epistemological theory was that of **science**, and has been labeled variously **empiricism**, **naturalism**, or **positivism**. Some of the specific assumptions of this epistemological theory are that there is a reality external to human beings; that this reality operates in a consistent fashion according to natural laws; and that this reality can be effectively explored through the human senses such as sight, smell, sound, and touch. Therefore, it is believed, human error in understanding the world can be overcome through certain methodological procedures such as **controlled experimentation**, manipulating and examining individual factors in a controlled and stable experimental environment where many factors can be held constant and only the experimental factor varied to see its effect, and **replication**, the repeating of experimental procedures in different venues by different researchers to see if there are consistent results.

Scientific epistemology had increasingly established itself since the Enlightenment in the eighteenth century, when science was first formulated as an alternative vision or paradigm to religion and knowledge according to holy scriptures and religious authorities (Greene 1959; Williams 1964). The success of science in the nineteenth and early twentieth centuries in revolutionizing understanding of the world and the impact of applied science and technology in transforming the world led many students of society, culture, and human life to adopt, partially or wholly, scientific epistemology.

Cultural anthropologists did not pursue scientific knowledge of human life like experimental chemists and physicists in laboratories, but rather like biologists and geologists in the field. For it was not specific procedures per se that defined scientific methodology, but the rigorous application of the logic of scientific inquiry in whatever venue of investigation. Anthropologists could not (and would not) vary the influence of culture by raising children in a laboratory, but anthropologists could and did examine the variation of culture by studying different cultures *in situ*, in their natural environments. Such comparisons were sometimes called "natural experiments," because the variation in influence and consequence—such as social discontinuity for teenagers in America and social continuity for teenagers in Samoa—existed in nature; and the research could collect the necessary information for answering a question and drawing a conclusion, for example, whether biological changes during puberty always lead to a disturbed adolescence, by observing the natural variations as they existed.

Many twentieth-century cultural anthropologists took science as a model of knowledge. Among these are two founders of British social anthropology, Bronislaw Malinowski, who published *A Scientific Theory of Culture* in 1944, and A. R. Radcliffe-Brown, who published *A Natural Science of Society* in 1948. S. F. Nadel's 1951 *The Foundations of Social Anthropology* was similarly inspired. Among influential contemporary American researchers, Marvin Harris begins his 1979 book *Cultural Materialism* by saying that "Cultural materialism is or aspires to be a scientific research strategy." Recent work by **evolutionary ecologists** (Cronk, Chagnon, and Irons 1999), among others, vigorously pursues scientific goals.

The social and cultural anthropologists taking a scientific approach envisioned a two-level discipline: there was ethnography, the study of particular, unique societies and cultures; and there was social and cultural anthropology, sometime called comparative anthropology or **ethnology**, which aimed at generalizations based upon the comparison or juxtaposition of two or more ethnographic cases. The kind of generalization these researchers had in mind was not so much **descriptive generalizations**, such as "Polynesian villagers do not have occupational choices" or "nomadic hunters live in small groups," but rather **theoretical generalizations**, another label for what I have called substantive theories, such as "social status continuity and fixed life courses result in emotionally smooth life course transitions, while social status discontinuity and many life course options result in emotionally disruptive life course transitions," and "among hunting peoples, the denser the resource base, the larger the social group, the more complex the social organization, and the more elaborate the culture."

Not all cultural and social anthropologists adopted a scientific model for anthropology. No less a figure than Franz Boas emphasized, as he phrased it in his foreword to *Coming of Age in Samoa*, the "endeavour to reconstruct, as well as may be, the history of each particular culture," and he was skeptical about the formulation of cross-cultural generalizations. So too E. E. Evans-Pritchard (1962:20–28), distinguished successor to Radcliffe-Brown, saw social anthropology as "a special kind of historiography," or history, and thus one of the humanities, and rejected the search for natural laws of society and culture. And the influential American Marxist anthropologist, Eric Wolf, emphasized historical analysis rather than theoretical generalization in his comparative works such as *Europe and the People without History* (1982). Some other anthropologists, such as the important American theorist Marshall Sahlins, who began with a scientific orientation and an interest in formulating theoretical generalizations, have shifted away from scientific generalization toward historical analysis, as we see in *Historical Metaphors and Mythical Realities* (1981) and subsequent works. But an elaborated alternative to scientific epistemology was not developed by the authors and did not emerge until the 1980s.

Postmodern anthropology has developed as a critique of scientific epistemology and offers an alternative vision of anthropological knowledge and anthropological objectives. Some of its main elements had been advocated by Evans-Pritchard (1962:22): The anthropologist, as ethnographer,

> lives among [a people] as intimately as he can, and he learns to speak their language, to think in their concepts and to feel in their values. He then lives the experiences over again critically and interpretatively in the conceptual categories and values of his own culture and in terms of the general body of knowledge of his discipline. In other words, he translates from one culture into another.

In this sense, social anthropology remains a literary and impressionistic art. Evans-Pritchard's stress on experience and interpretation rather than on observation, on literary translation rather than prediction, and on art rather than experiment, announces a break with science. And this is made even more explicit by Evans-Pritchard (1962:26).

> The thesis that I have put before you, that social anthropology is a kind of historiography, and therefore ultimately of philosophy or art, implies that it studies societies as moral systems and not as natural systems, that it is interested in design rather than in process, and that it therefore seeks patterns and not scientific laws, and interprets rather than explains.

A parallel approach was developed a decade later in America by Clifford Geertz. Geertz's rhetoric shifted away from the scientific paradigm as he identified, for the focus of anthropology, symbols and meaning rather than organization and behavior, or structure and function, which were the interests of more scientifically oriented anthropologists, and stressed the research processes of interpretation and translation, rather than the scientific ones of generalization and explanation. As he (1973:5) puts it in his groundbreaking collection, *The Interpretation of Cultures*,

> The concept of culture I espouse . . . is essentially a semiotic one. Believing, with Max Weber, that man is an animal suspended in webs of significance he himself has spun, I take culture to be those webs, and the analysis of it to be therefore not an experimental science in search of law but an interpretative one in search of meaning. It is explication I am after, construing social expressions on their surface enigmatical.

In other words, Geertz (1983:6, 58) is turning away from science and from

> trying to explain social phenomena by weaving them into grand textures of cause and effect to trying to explain them by placing

them in local frames of awareness . . . by searching out and analyz-
ing the symbolic forms—words, images, institutions, behaviors—in
terms of which, in each place, people actually represented themselves to themselves and to one another.

The formulation of this stance into a full, antiscience epistemology, taking to their logical conclusions—opponents would say logical
absurdity—the tenets of Evans-Pritchard and Geertz, waited until
1986, when the publication of *Anthropology As Cultural Critique* by
Marcus and Fischer, and *Writing Culture: The Poetics and Politics of
Ethnography*, by Clifford and Marcus, brought to life anthropological
postmodernism. Postmodern epistemology argues that anthropological
researchers, like everyone else, can only see and understand the world
through their own subjectivity, which is shaped by their own culture,
by the position that they inhabit in their own and international society,
and by their idiosyncratic makeup. Research is thus a process of subjective perception, in which the researcher interprets what he or she
sees, and then, in thinking, speaking, and writing about his or her subject people, constructs a picture or a story to represent the subject.
There are no facts, only interpretations. Because we can never see the
world except through our subjectivity, our interpretations will differ
from one another's. But there is no way to judge one from another in
terms of truth, because there are as many different truths as there are
observers. This postmodern epistemological theory thus stresses epistemological **relativity**, the idea that truth is not absolute, but relative
to one's perspective.

Following from this postmodern epistemological position is the
political implication that the anthropological researcher has no privileged position and her or his opinion has no special authority. On the
contrary, the authority is seen to be the privilege of the people studied,
who must be considered subjects and not objects of study, and whose
representation of themselves should be the prime information sought
by the ethnographer (Marcus 1994). The strong postmodern position is
that researchers have no right to construct and broadcast representations of a people; only that population can legitimately say who they
are. Thus there is an emphasis on the people studied expressing themselves in their own **voice**, and a disapprobation of any researcher who
steals the voice of his or her subjects. Finally, while from the postmodern epistemological perspective there is no truth that anthropologists
can discover, no substantive generalization or laws about society or culture that can legitimately be formulated, there are judgments that can
and must be made. Postmodern anthropologists believe that they are
obliged to take a moral stand, to side with the outcast, the oppressed,
the marginalized, and victims everywhere. So there is a shift of emphasis from the scientific objective of discovering something new and interesting about society and culture, to the postmodern objective of giving

the disadvantaged a voice and to **deconstructing** the culture of oppression by exposing its assumptions. In the postmodern perspective, an anthropological work cannot be judged as to whether it is true or false, but it can be judged as to whether it is relevant, socially responsible, and moral.

The scientific epistemological theory and the postmodern epistemological theory are alternative philosophical visions that have each been advocated and pursued by anthropologists throughout the 1990s. These different visions represent the major theoretical split among anthropologists at the turn of the millennium. Every discussion of culture theory today is conditioned by the debate among advocates of these opposing epistemological visions. Postmodern theory is a descendent of earlier, nonscientific or antiscientific anthropological approaches that emphasized historical development, culture patterns, and moral commitment.

SCHOOLS OF CULTURE THEORY

In discussing different theories of culture and the anthropologists who hold or advocate them—sometimes I will refer to those holding similar views as "schools," considered as loose and informal intellectual associations—I will base my primary categorization and labeling on the philosophical split between the scientific theorists and the non- or antiscientific theorists. As the scientific-minded aim for explanation in terms of cause and effect, and the nonscientific or humanistic (after the literary disciplines of the humanities) aim for explication in terms of meaning, I will divide culture theorists into two great camps: explanation and explication.

One of the basic differences between explanation and explication is the focus: **Explanation** is oriented toward **nomothetic** theories, which are general formulations about classes of facts or phenomena and which, in principle, would include all specific, individual cases that fall into that class. In other words, science aims at universal theories, each of which states a general truth about clearly specified classes of things, such as that nomadic hunters live in egalitarian groups, or that peasants never have strong, institutionalized leadership. The focus in explanation is thus characteristics shared by all individual cases (e.g., groups, societies, cultures) in the specified class (e.g., hunters, peasants). In contrast, **explication** is oriented toward **idiographic** formulations, statements about unique, particular cases such as specific cultures, communities, groups, developmental sequences, and patterns of contact.

Within the camp of explanation, I will distinguish and discuss different theories in terms of their bases of explanation: functionalist interdependence (chapter 2), processualist agency (chapter 3), and materialist determinism (chapter 4). Within the camp of explication, I will distinguish between different theories in terms of their field of interest: culture patterns (chapter 5), history and evolution (chapter 6), and moral judgment (chapter 7). Our discussion will conclude with a reflection on anthropological theory (chapter 8) that integrates the material covered by presenting the arguments and debates among the various theoretical positions.

A caution: In the course of presenting the various theoretical perspectives, ethnographic examples used by authors—about African witchcraft, Indian cattle, Roman ritual, South American rubber collectors, Persian nomads, and Australian totems, among many others—are summarized here to illustrate and exemplify the ways in which the theories are applied. However, the ethnographic "facts" and interpretations presented in any case may be controversial and not accepted by all specialists, and in some cases may have been superseded by new formulations since the authors originally published their accounts. The ethnographic cases presented in this volume are thus intended primarily to illustrate a theoretical approach and should not be taken by the reader as the authoritative or final word on the people or practice described.

Additional material includes a glossary of terms, a list of important authors and their works, and references for further reading.

Chapter Two

Interdependence in Human Life
Social Structure and Function

Zechariah, a member of the Cewa people of Zambia in southern Africa, was accused of sorcery (Marwick 1965:219, Case No. 26). Here is why:

> Zechariah betrothed a girl and then went to work in Southern Rhodesia [now Zimbabwe]. After he had been there three years, the girl said, 'How's this? When he left me, I was but a child. Now I am a grown woman. Now I'll form a liaison with a man.' This she proceeded to do, with Abelo. Zechariah received a letter from his sister in which she reported the infidelity of his betrothed; and he wrote back to her, 'How is it that my betrothed has taken on with Abelo? She will see [i.e. experience] something!' And he signed his letter with the drawing of a lion. After a month, lions came and took one of Abelo's beasts. Next day they caught another; and on the following day, yet another. But when the lions came to catch Abelo himself, they failed to get him, and went back again to Southern Rhodesia where they were received by their master [Zechariah]. Zechariah now procured 'medicines' which he sent through the air, and with them he killed Abelo's mother, three of his sisters, two of his mother's sisters, two of his younger brothers, his mother's mother and his mother's brother. The accuser, Abelo, did not need to make enquiries; to him it was obvious who the sorcerer was.

How do anthropologists explain sorcery and witchcraft? First of all, most anthropologists, particularly those who hold to a scientific epistemology, do not believe in the existence of sorcery and witchcraft powers and acts. So what anthropologists want to explain is beliefs in sorcery and witchcraft, which can be seen as cultural facts, and accusations of sorcery and witchcraft, which are social facts. Here is how anthropologists, particularly British social anthropologists of mid-century who carried out much research on this subject, have explained beliefs in sorcery and witchcraft and accusations against alleged practitioners.

British social anthropologists have explained sorcery and witchcraft by drawing attention to their consequences, or **functions**. Sorcery and witchcraft do a number of important things in small, face-to-face communities such as the African villages of the Cewa. First, sorcery and witchcraft explain unfortunate events, such as the illness of a particular person, which, in terms of local knowledge, cannot be explained as natural phenomena (Evans-Pritchard 1937; Marwick 1965:281–82). Second, explaining unfortunate events in terms of sorcery and witchcraft moralizes natural causality by using disturbances in social relations to explain the course of events and especially misfortune (Marwick 1965:281). By moralizing natural causality, sorcery and witchcraft beliefs and accusations dramatize social norms and rules, positioning the (alleged) sorcerer or witch as an evil, antisocial criminal (Marwick 1965:245). Finally, accusations overtly expressed social conflict and negative feelings that had been hidden in people's hearts, thus opening the opportunity for repair of social relationships or, alternatively, for a reordering of social relationships (Marwick 1965:283; Turner 1957).

This example of the anthropological explanation of sorcery and witchcraft introduces us to one of the foundation theories of modern anthropology: the **functionalist** or **structural functionalist** heuristic theory.

Beginning early in the twentieth century and dominating British social anthropology until around 1960, with strong influence in America and elsewhere, the functionalist or structural functionalist paradigm or model or vision was the most coherent and perhaps most formative heuristic theory in modern anthropology. Its founders were Bronislaw Malinowski and A. R. Radcliffe-Brown.

The most basic tenets of the functionalist heuristic theory are these: Each society consists of a number of distinguishable parts, established patterns of organization, activity, and value—such as matrilineal descent groups, or age sets, or divine kingships, or witchcraft detectives, or ancestor worship—which were variously called **institutions** or **structures** of social relations. Malinowski ([1944] 1960:52–53) defined an institution as "an organized system of purposeful activities" that included a "charter," such as a myth or history or formal agreement, that defines the "personnel," both who is included and the relationships among them, and also the "norms," or rules that people must follow, the "material apparatus," including tools and materials, that is used in the set "activities," and the "function" that is filled by those activities. According to Malinowski ([1944] 1960:40), each culture can be understood as an integrated whole of "partly autonomous, partly coordinated institutions." Radcliffe-Brown (1952:190–92; article originally published in 1940) focused more specifically on the "complex network of social relations," which he called "social structure," including all "actually existing relations."

> In the first place, I regard as a part of the social structure all social relations of person to person. For example, the kinship structure of any society consists of a number of such dyadic relations, as between a father and son, or a mother's brother and his sister's son. . . .
>
> Secondly, I include under social structure the differentiation of individuals and of classes by their social role. The differential social positions of men and women, of chiefs and commoners, of employers and employees, are just as much determinants of social relations as belonging to different clans or different nations.

These institutions and structures had not only content—such as political activities by the king, the search for witches, or ownership of horticultural land—but also consequences, or functions, for the other institutions and structures in the society and for the society as a whole. In the words of Radcliffe-Brown (1952:180; article originally published in 1935),

> The *function* of any recurrent activity, such as the punishment of a crime, or a funeral ceremony, is the part it plays in the social life as a whole and therefore the contribution it makes to the maintenance of the structural continuity.

This concept of function was drawn by Radcliffe-Brown (1952:178; article originally published in 1935) from the work of Emile Durkheim, a founder of French sociology and anthropology. "Function" and other ideas important to British social anthropology are discussed in *The Division of Labor in Society* (1933; published originally in 1893 under the title *De la division du travail social*). Malinowski, in some of his work, especially *A Scientific Theory of Culture*, emphasized the way in which institutions function to satisfy universal, biological needs such as metabolism, reproduction, safety, etc., but this focus was not favored by most of his contemporaries.

What kind of specific social function could various cultural practices have? To take one example, ancestor worship gave supernatural support to the structure of matrilineal descent groups. It did this because descent groups were based on descent from common ancestors, and ancestor worship recognized the ancestors of descent groups as supernatural powers. This meant that to violate descent group rules, to not fulfill one's group obligations, was to risk supernatural punishment by the deceased ancestors of the group. So one of the functions of ancestor worship was to reinforce the authority and the rules of the lineage groups.

Thus, to understand the way a society worked, functionalists searched for the impact that each custom or practice had on an institution or structure, and the impact that each institution or structure had on every other institution or structure. In other words, they focused on the interdependence of the customs and practices, structures and institutions in a society, the way in which each custom and practice, institution and structure in a society had been shaped by and was dependent on the existence of the others.

FUNCTIONALISM AND ETHNOGRAPHIC FIELD RESEARCH

Structural functionalist theory arose in the first decades of the twentieth century together with a new mode of conducting ethnographic research: long-term fieldwork utilizing participant observation. **Participant observation** includes such activities as attending rituals and ceremonies, going to the fields and pastures and fishing areas to watch and even help with production activities, sitting in on court cases, following political deliberations, engaging in play and sports activities, and listening and even entering into discussions, debates, and arguments, as well as having informal conversations with local people, holding formal interviews, doing surveys, and collecting oral knowledge and written documents.

In the nineteenth century, most anthropologists were either "armchair" researchers, living in their home countries and relying for information about distant societies and their customs, practices, and beliefs on reports from government officials, missionaries, and travelers, or they were short-term expeditionary travelers who made very brief visits to survey distant societies, collecting some information and some artifacts, then quickly moving to another site or returning home. In the early twentieth century, anthropologists began to live for extended periods in distant societies, studying the local way of life firsthand through direct observation and sometimes active participation. Instead of communicating through interpreters or pidgin languages, these new anthropologists in their roles as field ethnographers settled down to learn the local languages so that they could communicate in the vernacular of the people they were studying and could understand the local people as they went about their own business (Stocking 1992:ch. 1).

These new fieldwork ethnographers, living in the communities that they were studying, were able to follow local activities as they developed from one event to another, and saw the changes in life as one season succeeded another through the year. They spent a lot of time with local people and got to know at least some of them fairly well. This is how Malinowski ([1922] 1984:7), whose fieldwork in the Trobriand

Islands in Melanesia (Western Pacific) set the modern standard (cp. Stocking 1992:ch. 1), describes his experience:

> Soon after I had established myself in Omarakana (Trobriand Islands), I began to take part, in a way, in the village life, to look forward to the important or festive events, to take personal interest in the gossip and the developments of the small village occurrences; to wake up every morning to a day, presenting itself to me more or less as it does to the native. . . . As I went on my morning walk through the village, I could see intimate details of family life, of toilet, cooking, taking of meals; I could see the arrangements for the day's work, people starting on their errands, or groups of men and women busy at some manufacturing tasks. Quarrels, jokes, family scenes, events usually trivial, sometimes dramatic but always significant, formed the atmosphere of my daily life, as well as of theirs. . . .
>
> Later on in the day, whatever happened was within easy reach, and there was no possibility of its escaping my notice. Alarms about the sorcerer's approach in the evening, one or two big, really important quarrels and rifts within the community, cases of illness, attempted cures and deaths, magical rites which had to be performed, all these I had not to pursue, fearful of missing them, but they took place under my very eyes, at my own doorstep, so to speak.

Malinowski ([1922] 1984:21) watched and observed, but he also joined in, participating in various activities of local life.

> . . . [I]n this type of work, it is good for the Ethnographer sometimes to put aside camera, note book and pencil, and to join in himself in what is going on. He can take part in the natives' games, he can follow them on their visits and walks, sit down and listen and share in their conversations. . . . Out of such plunges into the life of the natives—and I made them frequently not only for study's sake but because everyone needs human company—I have carried away a distinct feeling that their behaviour, that their manner of being, in all sorts of tribal transactions, became more transparent and easily understandable than it had been before.

Through this extended residence and participant observation, anthropologists were able to explore fully—by means of direct observation of activities, conversations, and surveys and reviews of documents—various subjects of interest, such as how people raise and teach and discipline their children, or whether people believe in witches and under what circumstances they accuse people of being witches, or what material necessities or ritual objects people trade with one another, and with whom, or how the gender roles and status are defined, and how men and women get along, or whether and how some people are vested with authority to make decisions, and what decisions they make.

Once armed with information on practices and beliefs in various specific fields, or institutions, of social life, such as child rearing, religion, gender, politics, and so forth, functionalists would examine the interrelations between these fields. How did child rearing affect gender roles and relations? How did religion interact with child rearing and with gender? In what way did religion contribute to political roles and structures, and how did politics support religious practice and belief? Discovering **functional interrelations** between various customs and institutions was the way in which functionalists explained these customs and institutions.

Basing anthropological research on ethnographic fieldwork led to reports of findings about the society and culture studied called **ethnographies**, which were largely **synchronic** in form. That is, they presented a picture of the society and culture at a moment in time, the time that the ethnographers were present and observing the society. It was characteristic to present descriptions of kin relations, or religion, or politics as **systems**, that is, as a number of interrelated parts, the system and the parts of each system having structures, specific arrangements of the parts, and having functions, interrelations with and consequences for the other parts and the other systems in the society. There was not much **diachronic** reporting, at least in the ethnographies during the 1920s and 1930s, of historical perspectives on these societies and their institutions, not much about changes and developments in these customs and practices and beliefs over time.

There were two practical reasons for the emphasis on synchronic ethnographic studies. One was that researchers seldom were able to reside at their field sites for periods of more than a year or two, so did not have the opportunity to see changes over ten or twenty or more years. The other was that in many of the societies studied early on, such as hunting and cultivating societies, literacy was absent or only recent, and so there were no archives of historical documents about earlier periods.

There was also a theoretical reason for emphasis on synchronic research. Some previous researchers, especially those with an evolutionary bent, had engaged, in the absence of historical records, in elaborate speculations about the historical origins of cultural customs and practices (Radcliffe-Brown 1952:3; Kuper 1988). This led the structural functionalists to criticize historical conjecture and undisciplined imagination and to reject "pseudo-historical" explanations (Radcliffe-Brown 1952:3). In the place of these faulty approaches, Radcliffe-Brown (1948, 1952) wanted to establish a scientific anthropology based upon direct observations and empirical evidence. This was seen as a more valid basis of knowledge, but in many cases restricted the knowledge to synchronic accounts.

Let us explore the theoretical formulations of the functionalists by examining, in turn, four examples by prominent researchers, A. R. Radcliffe-Brown, Bronislaw Malinowski, S. F. Nadel, and Max Gluckman.

EXPLAINING THE ROLE OF
THE MOTHER'S BROTHER

When we think about **kinship**, we usually imagine that we are referring to biology, to insemination and parturition, to blood and to genes. So do people in other cultures. However, it became quickly clear to anthropologists that, in spite of the biological referent in people's minds, kinship is really a **cultural idiom**, that is, a way of speaking and thinking learned by people in each culture. The proof is that kinship—including kinship terminology, who is categorized with whom and who distinguished from whom and how they are labeled, and kinship organization, how people are grouped together or separated in social groups—differs from place to place, often in very striking ways. One clear-cut example is that people in many societies say that they are descended only from their mothers, grandmothers, and great-grandmothers, that is, through the female line, while people in many other societies say that they are descended only from their fathers, grandfathers, and great-grandfathers. For our part, we of course believe that we are descended from both our mother's and father's sides. This difference in beliefs about descent could not result from biological differences, because human beings share a common biology, with only a few tiny differences. Thus the striking differences in kinship from society to society must result from differences in culture.

Another example of differences in kinship from society to society is the way in which the brothers and sisters, siblings, of parents are thought of. While North Americans of European extraction treat parents' siblings alike, calling parents' brothers "uncle" and parents' sisters "aunt," in many other cultures mother's brothers and sisters are called one thing and father's brothers and sisters called something else. Not only that, but in these societies the rules of expected behavior between a person and his or her mother's siblings are different from the rules about a person and her or his father's siblings. How can we explain that? This is the subject of an early paper of Radcliffe-Brown (1952:ch. 1; paper originally presented in 1924), which demonstrates the (then) new mode of functionalist thinking and shows how customs and institutions are explained by the functionalists.

Radcliffe-Brown pointed to the highly indulgent relationship between a sister's son (ZS) and his mother's brother (MB) found among the BaThonga of southeast Africa, in Tonga, in Polynesia, in Fiji, and in many other societies. The MB takes his ZS under special care and is always looking out for him. When the ZS is sick, the MB sacrifices on his behalf. The MB allows the ZS to come into his house and eat the food prepared for his own meal, as well as allowing him to take the meat or beer that MB offers to his ancestors. The ZS may claim some of the property of his deceased MB, including even one of his widows. Among the Nama Hottentots of southern Africa, the ZS may take any particularly fine cow or bull, or other object, of the MB.

This custom, the close and indulgent relationship between MB and ZS, is explained by some evolutionist authors (cited by Radcliffe-Brown, ibid) as reflecting mother-right, including descent through the female line, or **matrilineality**. But as the groups under consideration by Radcliffe-Brown had, during the period of research, a strong father-right, or **patrilineality**, the custom of ZS rights in the property of the MB was deemed (by these earlier evolutionist authors) to reflect an earlier historical stage in which these groups were matrilineal and had a dominant mother-right, in which property passed along the female line, from the MB to the ZS. Radcliffe-Brown objects to this evolutionary theory, partly on the theoretical grounds that it is totally speculative and lacking any direct evidence to support it.

Radcliffe-Brown (ibid) also objects to the evolutionary theory on the ethnographic grounds that another customary kinship pattern present in these same societies, and apparently related to the MB-ZS indulgent relationship, is not explained by the hypothesized earlier state of mother-right. This related pattern is the highly severe, rigidly respectful relationship between the father's sister (FZ) and the brother's son (BS). Radcliffe-Brown argues that there is no basis for such a relationship in a system of mother-right or matrilineality, in which the father and the father's sister are in a different group from the son, have no authority over the son, and are more likely to be indulgent than strict. Therefore, he argued, the severe FZ-BS relationship found in these societies is not explained by a hypothesized earlier stage of mother-right.

Radcliffe-Brown (ibid) offers a different hypothesis to serve as an explanation. In these societies members of each descent group—those people united by descent from a common ancestor—are treated in an undifferentiated manner, as being socially equivalent. From the point of view of an individual in a patrilineal society, mother and MB are the members of one line and group, a group other than one's own; similarly, father and FZ are members of one line and one group, the group to which one does belong. Consequently, MB is like a male mother, and FZ is treated as a female father, as is in some societies indicated by the kin terms. In these patrilineal societies, duty and discipline rest with the senior members of one's own group, that is, with one's father and father's patrilineal kin, including FZ. Nurturing and support come from one's other relatives, mother and MB and the patrilineal members of their descent group, of which one is not a member and to which one has no obligations. The indulgent MB-ZS relationship and the severe BS-FZ relationship are therefore best understood, according to Radcliffe-

Brown, as social roles functionally interdependent with the patrilineal system of descent and group formation.

This example illustrates the general functionalist principle, as stated by Radcliffe-Brown (1952:17), that to explain customs and institutions we must relate them "to other institutions with which they coexist and with which they may be correlated." What **correlated** means is that the institutions go together; that is, they are tied together and each does not appear without the other. So that if one is found, we can **predict** that the other one is present. On the other hand, if one is absent, we can predict that the other one is absent. This is how Radcliffe-Brown constructs his hypothesis about the indulgent MB-ZS and severe FZ-BS relationships. He says they are found in societies with strong father-right, including descent, inheritance, and succession through the male line, as well as residence with or near the father. The other side of the hypothesis is that the indulgent MB-ZS and severe FZ-BS relationships will not be found in societies with strong mother-right or with balanced but weaker influence by both mother's and father's sides.

Radcliffe-Brown elaborated his theory in essays such as "On the Concept of Function in Social Science" (1952:ch. 9; originally published in 1935) and "On Social Structure" (1952:ch. 10, originally published in 1940), which appear in his collection *Structure and Function in Primitive Society* (1952). The "Introduction" to that volume offers some final formulations and orientations.

UNDERSTANDING RELIGIOUS RITUALS

Religious rituals that have appeared mysterious, amazing, horrifying, and astonishing to outsiders were early discovered in anthropology. Sir James Frazier, the famous nineteenth-century English anthropologist, began his monumental, twelve-volume survey of cultures, *The Golden Bough*, by describing a ritual at the "little woodland lake of Nemi," in the Alban hills of central Italy ([1890] 1960:1).

> In antiquity this sylvan landscape was the scene of a strange and recurring tragedy. . . . [In the sacred grove and sanctuary of Diana of the Wood] there grew a certain tree round which at any time of day, and probably far into the night, a grim figure might be seen to prowl. In his hand he carried a drawn sword, and he kept peering warily about him as if at every instant he expected to be set upon by an enemy. He was a priest and a murderer; and the man for whom he looked was sooner or later to murder him and hold the priesthood in his stead. Such was the rule of the sanctuary. A candidate for the priesthood could only succeed to office by slaying the priest, and having slain him, he retained office till he was himself slain by a stronger or a craftier.

Twentieth-century anthropologists, stimulated by what they had observed during their firsthand ethnographic fieldwork, have been equally fascinated by religious ritual and have taken pains to explain ritual by application of their theoretical frameworks. Malinowski addressed religion and ritual in his essay "Magic, Science and Religion" ([1925] 1992). There he (pp. 17, 38) made his well-known distinctions between "the Sacred and the Profane; in other words, the domain of Magic and Religion and that of Science," and between magic, which is goal oriented, and religion, which is an end in itself:

> While in the magical act the underlying idea and aim is always clear, straight-forward and definite, in the religious ceremony there is not purpose directed toward a subsequent event. . . . The native can always state the end of the magical rite, but he will say of a religious ceremony that it is done because such is the usage, or because it has been ordained, or he will narrate an explanatory myth.

Among the religious ceremonies discussed by Malinowski are those that take place at life changes such as birth and death, sometimes called by anthropologists **life cycle rituals** or *rites de passage*. Malinowski ([1925] 1992:38–40) addresses, among other life cycle rituals, ceremonies of initiation. These rites are widespread among tribal peoples and are well known from North American, Australian, Melanesian, and other societies. Common features found in these ceremonies are the following: First, there is a period of seclusion and preparation. This often involves removing the initiates from their homes and communities and locating them in some isolated place. There they are given instruction from elders about secret tribal knowledge. Second, there is the formal initiation ritual involving one or a series of ordeals, usually involving bodily mutilation, anything from minor cuts or the removal of a tooth, to radical genital mutilation in Australian subincision, the slicing open of the penis along its length.

These ritual events bring the initiate under the power of tribal culture heroes, guardian spirits or gods, who are thought to transform, or to kill and restore, the initiate, returning him as a fully initiated man. Superior and superhuman forces are represented by ritual apparatus such as the Australian bull-roarer, the hum of which is understood to be the voice of the tribal all-father. The completed passing into manhood brings the initiation ritual to a close.

Why do these elaborated and seemingly exaggerated ceremonies exist? Malinowski ([1925] 1992:37) suggests that we seek the answer not in the substance of the local beliefs or activities, but in the social function of the rituals. "Since we cannot define cult and creed by their objects, perhaps it will be possible to perceive their function." In other words, we can understand the existence of these ceremonial activities by seeing how they contribute to the society in which they are embedded;

"what is the sociological function of these customs, what part do they play in the maintenance and development of civilization?" (pp. 39–40).

What, then, is the function of initiation ceremonies? Malinowski (Ibid.) argues that, in these tribal societies,

> tradition is of supreme value for the community and nothing matters as much as the conformity and conservatism of its members. Order and civilization can be maintained only by strict adhesion to the lore and knowledge received from previous generations. Any laxity in this weakens the cohesion of the group and imperils its cultural outfit to the point of threatening its very existence. . . . [A] society which makes its tradition sacred has gained by it an inestimable advantage of power and permanence. Such beliefs and practices, therefore, which put a halo of sanctity round tradition and a supernatural stamp upon it, will have a "survival value" for the type of civilization in which they have been evolved.

Initiation rites put this stamp of sacredness on tribal tradition at the same time as it passes that tradition on to the next generation. The intense experience of separation from ordinary life and of encounter with pain and suffering brands the mind of the initiate with the importance of both the tribal knowledge learned and the new status and responsibilities: "the light of tribal revelation bursts upon him from out of the shadows of fear, privation, and bodily pain" (p. 39). Malinowski (p. 40) thusly sums up the main functions of initiation ceremonies:

> [T]hey are a ritual and dramatic expression of the supreme power and value of tradition in primitive societies; they also serve to impress this power and value upon the minds of each generation, and they are at the same time an extremely efficient means of transmitting tribal lore, of insuring continuity in tradition and of maintaining tribal cohesion.

For Malinowski, as a functionalist theorist, initiation rites in their many variations and manifestations could best be understood in their contribution to the maintenance of tradition in tribal societies that depended upon universal conformity for their continuation and survival.

WHO ARE THE WITCHES?

Let us return to the topic of sorcery and witchcraft with a comparative study by S. F. Nadel, "Witchcraft in Four African Societies" (1952), in which Nadel compares first two societies to one another, and then two others to each other. Nadel notes that patterns of witchcraft accusation are quite different in different societies. He wants to explain why one pattern of accusation exists in one society and a different one in another. His theoretical assumption is that "any one relevant cultural divergence entails further, concomitant, divergences in the respective cultures." Concomitant means that things go together and change together, that they **co-vary**, and that therefore they are correlated. Nadel will explain the differences in patterns of witchcraft accusation by comparing the patterns in two societies, citing other differences in the two societies compared. He characterizes this as an analysis of **concomitant variations**.

What is Nadel's substantive theory that will guide him in searching for explanations of the witchcraft accusation patterns? He argues that "witchcraft beliefs are causally related to frustrations, anxieties or other mental stresses" and therefore that difficult social relationships that lead to frustrations, anxieties, or other mental stresses will, in African tribal societies, generate witchcraft accusations. If witchcraft accusation patterns differ between two societies, it is—according to this hypothesis—because stress is found in different social relationships in the two societies.

Two societies that Nadel compares are Nupe and Gwari, geographical neighbors in northern Nigeria. Now it is no accident that these two societies are close by and have many similar features such as environment, patrilineal kinship system, political organization, religion, and a conception of witchcraft as a life-destroying evil in which witches use wasting diseases to eat the life-soul of their victims. Nadel has chosen to compare these two societies because their many commonalities make it easy to identify those factors that differ between the two societies. A variable, such as differences in witchcraft accusations, cannot be explained by a constant, such as a similar environment in these two societies. The more constants (called in scientific terminology "controls" or "controlled variables") present in the two cases, the easier it is to find the one or two variables that co-vary with, and thus are correlated with, the variable to be explained.

One difference between the Nupe and Gwari, and the thing that Nadel wishes to explain (in scientific terminology, the "dependent variable"), is the pattern of witchcraft accusations. Among the Nupe, accusations of witchcraft are always directed at women, usually an older and domineering female, and never at men, and young men are regarded as the main victims of witchcraft. Nadel (1952:19) recounts a case history:

> . . . [A] young man from a village on the river Niger . . . one night suddenly disappeared. A body which the police had good reason to believe was his was later fished out of the river; but the people refused to accept this "natural" explanation, maintaining that the young man had been spirited away by a witch. Suspicion at once fell on an elderly wealthy woman whose house the young man had frequently been visiting; he had, in fact, been something like a protege of that woman. . . .

Among the Gwari, the pattern of witchcraft accusations is quite distinct from that among the Nupe. Witchcraft accusations are directed against both males and females, and both females and males are regarded to be victims of witchcraft.

How can this difference in witchcraft accusations between Nupe and Gwari be explained? Nadel relates this to the difference in marriage relations in the two societies: Marriage ties are "without serious complications and relatively tension-free in Gwari, but full of stress and mutual hostility in Nupe." These differences in marriage relations arise from differences in economic activities. The men in both Gwari and Nupe are cultivators, and the Gwari women remain in this sphere. In contrast, many Nupe women have become successful itinerant (traveling) traders, gaining considerable wealth and independence. They are able to dominate the men financially and to live morally lax lives away from home. Some also refuse to have children. The rejection of motherhood and the life of laxity is seen by the men as a great immorality, which weighs on top of the economic domination by the women. The frustration of the men and the hostility between the men and the women lead the men to think of women as attacking witches, and to think of themselves as victims. The witchcraft accusations by the men against the women reflect the antagonism between the men and the women, as well as the practical weakness of the men to alter the activities of the women.

In this comparison of Nupe and Gwari societies, Nadel identifies a concomitant variation, or co-variation, or correlation, between the variables witchcraft accusation patterns, on the one hand, and marital relationships, on the other. As marital relations (in scientific terminology, the "independent variable") vary from tension-free in Gwari to hostile in Nupe, so witchcraft accusation (the "dependent variable") varies from gender-unrelated among the Gwari to gender-oriented among the Nupe. Similarly, marital relations between the two societies co-vary in relation to economic activities; good gender relations among the Gwari are related to wives and husbands working together, and hostile gender relations among the Nupe are related to wives working and living independently away from their husband and families and giving priority to their work. (Are there any parallels with gender relations in North American society?)

Nadel also develops a comparison between two other societies, the neighboring tribes of Korongo and Mesakin of the Nuba mountains in central Sudan, which turns on conflict and witchcraft accusations over anticipated inheritance by sister's son (ZS) from mother's brother (MB) in a matrilineal organization (pretty much the opposite of the ZS-MB relationship in patrilineal societies, just as Radcliffe-Brown would have predicted). He (1952:27–28) then draws his conclusions, among which are the following:

The witchcraft beliefs here examined are causally as well as conspicuously related to specific anxieties and stresses arising in social life. The word "conspicuously" is relevant because the witchcraft beliefs also indicate the precise nature of the social causes of which they are the symptoms—marriage-relations in Nupe, and the relationship between mother's-brother and sister's son in Mesakin. . . .

The witchcraft fears and accusations only accentuate concrete hostilities and in fact give them free rein. . . . [But at the same time] accusations of witchcraft *do* deflect tensions and aggressive impulses; these are deflected, as it were, from the maladjusted institutions which cause them—marriage and the economic system in Nupe, kinship relations and the regulation of adolescence in Mesakin—so that these institutions can continue to operate. But they remain maladjusted and their continued operation only creates further tensions.

Nadel thus shows not only how witchcraft, marriage, and economy are functionally interrelated, but also that witchcraft accusations, by acting as an emotional escape valve, allow the flawed institutions of Nupe marriage and Mesakin age organization to be maintained, unchallenged and unreformed. Thus Nadel explains the maintenance and continuity of Nupe marriage and Mesakin age organization. Not that he thinks this continuity is a particularly good thing; he calls it "a poor and ineffectual palliative," when really some "radical readjustment" is called for. Explanation of certain things in the world, which is the primary job of the anthropologist, is not necessarily justification of those things.

Nadel uses **comparative analysis** as a **methodological strategy** to search for concomitant variations, or correlations, on which he can base his explanations. The co-variation he finds in his comparisons then provide a basis for general explanation, a substantive, theoretical generalization, that "witchcraft beliefs . . . are causally . . . related to specific anxieties and stresses arising in social life." This theoretical generalization can then serve as an hypothesis in examining other cases of witchcraft accusations. With an accumulation of studies supporting this hypothesis, the generalization becomes established as valid theoretical knowledge. Negative cases, which appear to refute the hypothesis, would require a reassessment and either a reformulation of the hypothesis to accommodate the divergent cases or outright rejection of the hypothetical generalization. (In contrast to Nadel's comparisons of two closely related cases, some other anthropologists [e.g., Murdock 1949] have done broad ranging, even worldwide comparisons, in the pursuit of generalizations.)

Nadel's attention to the methodological strategy by which we gain scientific knowledge of human life, society, and culture is reflected in his book *The Foundations of Social Anthropology* (1951:v), about which he says, "The book, then, is about *Method*." As we have seen, research and analytical methods, on the one hand, and theory, on the other, are closely intertwined, or, as functionalists would happily put it, functionally interdependent.

THE PEACE IN THE FEUD

How is it that people cooperate and stick together in social groups over time and in the face of many difficulties, even though they may have divergent or conflicting individual interests? This question, called the problem of social cohesion, has been a central puzzle of sociology and anthropology since the nineteenth century. Emile Durkheim ([1893] 1933; Lukes 1972) argued that there are two distinct fashions in which people are drawn together, two distinct bases of social cohesion: **mechanical solidarity** and **organic solidarity**.

Mechanical solidarity is found in tribal societies made up of segments such as villages, clans, or lineages that are very much like one another, the people in different segments having the same occupations, growing the same crops and raising the same animals, and producing the same products. According to Durkheim ([1893] 1933), in such **segmentary** societies, there is little social or economic interdependence, for everyone has just about the same material goods as everyone else. What holds these societies together is a strong collective identity and common culture, called by Durkheim the *conscience collective*, which includes full sets of definite and specific social rules that everyone must follow, strong social and supernatural sanctions, or punishments, for those who violate the rules, and a commitment to the overriding importance of the collectivity as a whole. In other words, it is their cultural commonality and collective consciousness that holds segmentary societies together.

Organic solidarity, according the Durkheim ([1893] 1933), is found in societies with advanced technology, cities, literacy, and markets. In these societies there is a strong division of labor, with different groups specialized in different tasks: some growing crops, some extracting raw materials, some manufacturing goods, some transporting crops and goods, some providing services. As a result, there is pervasive **interdependence** among individuals and groups, each depending on all others for the goods and services needed and desired. In societies based on organic solidarity, social solidarity arises from practical interdependence, even though culture and identity are more variable, rules are less restrictive and aim toward compensation rather than punishment, and the individual and values of justice are emphasized.

Durkheim relied for his information on historical documentation and ethnographic secondary sources. When later anthropologists did direct research, ethnographic fieldwork, among segmentary tribal peoples, they too asked how these societies of like parts held together. Max Gluckman, reflecting on this research in *Custom and Conflict in Africa* (1959:ch. 1), discovered social arrangements not known by Durkheim that functioned to maintain peace and unity in segmentary societies. Here is Gluckman's (1959:2) general thesis:

> . . . men quarrel in terms of certain of their customary allegiances, but are restrained from violence through other conflicting allegiances which are also enjoined on them by custom. The result is that conflicts in one set of relationships, over a wider range of society or through a longer period of time, lead to the re-establishment of social cohesion.

Many segmentary tribal societies are **acephalous**, headless, in that there is no hierarchical, governmental structure, no chiefs or kings or judges. Rather, political rights and responsibilities, such as decision making and the application of force, are decentralized among the entire population. In practice, this usually means that household heads consult with household members and with each other, and come to collective decisions through discussion, debate, negotiation, and compromise. Commonly, as amongst the Nuer of the southern Sudan (Evans-Pritchard 1940) used by Gluckman to illustrate his thesis, individuals are members of groups—in this case **lineage** groups based on common descent through male ancestors—which have a collective responsibility to protect their members and their members' property, and to take vengeance or receive compensation in case of harm to one of their members. Groups so charged with responsibility for security are the main agents of **social control**, which includes all customary or institutionalized measures such as rules of vengeance and of compensation, ensuring order in the society. In such segmentary tribes—which also include the Maasai of East Africa (Spear and Waller 1993), the Somali of the Horn of Africa (Lewis 1961), the Bedouin of Arabia (Lancaster [1981] 1997), and the Turkmen of Central Asia (Irons 1975)—every man (excepting the few religious officials) is a warrior and must be ready to fight.

Where society consists of these separate groups of fighters, what keeps the society from breaking down into a multitude of tiny, warring nations? And what difference would it make? It would make a lot of difference if every little group were fighting every other little group, because peace over geographical space and through time is needed for people to sow and reap their crops and to herd their livestock; some degree of peaceful stability is necessary for people to make a living. But, as Gluckman (1959:9) points out, things do not happen because they are beneficial, but because specific arrangements exist to bring them about. These arrangements in segmentary societies are conflicting allegiances and divided loyalties. What happens is that people who are members of groups charged with security and that must be ready to engage in military combat with other such groups, have important relationships with individual members of enemy (or potentially enemy) groups. These allegiances with enemy individuals conflict with allegiance to the security group and divide loyalty, and thus lead individuals to press, in any dispute and potential combat, for compromise and compensation, for reason and reconciliation.

Gluckman (1959:ch. 1) points out that there are among the Nuer many allegiances conflicting with the patrilineal security group. The lineages that serve as security groups are not compact local groups but are always to a degree dispersed, with some members living in one community and others living in others. Thus members of different security groups live together in the same local communities, where they cooperate and work together and owe each other consideration and support. There is therefore a potential conflict of allegiance and divided loyalty between a Nuer man and the members of his local community, on the one hand, and between that Nuer man and his dispersed patrilineage, on the other. In a conflict between his lineage and another lineage with members in his own community, he will have strong moral and practical reasons for pressing for a timely and smooth settlement and for opposing belligerence and violence.

And while one kind of kinship, unilineal descent, underlies the formation of the security groups, other kinds of kinship, lateral ties through a Nuer male's mother and affinal ties through his wife, establish close and important ties with individuals from other lineage security groups. This is not primarily a result of individual choices and preferences; rather it is a consequence of customary rules of Nuer culture. A Nuer has strong customary obligations to aid and assist his sisters' sons, and he also has the ability to sanction them severely by means of supernatural curse. A Nuer man thus has a strong tie with his mother's brother. Because the Nuer rule of marriage is **exogamy**, or marriage outside of the group, a man's mother's brother always belongs to a different lineage than he does, and so he has a major investment in a potentially enemy lineage. As the Nuer rule of exogamy extends beyond one's lineage to all of one's relatives, for example, mother's lineage, Nuer in any lineage will be related to and married to people from a wide range of other lineages, spreading a **cross-cutting**, matrilateral and affinal **network** widely across lineage security groups. In almost any conflict between Nuer security groups, some members of those security groups will have important ties with members of the enemy group. They will therefore press for a peaceful settlement and the reestablishment of cordial ties between the groups. This is, as Gluckman puts it, the peace in the feud.

Gluckman's argument implies that, contra-Durkheim, peace and security do not arise from similarity alone, and unity cannot be posited but must be explained. Gluckman presents a more specific, structural theory based upon more detailed ethnography than Durkheim had at his disposal: Customary cultural rules, such as the basing of security groups on the nonspatial principle of descent and the basing of marriage on exogamy, lead for each individual to cross-cutting social allegiances and conflicting political loyalties, which function to diffuse political conflict, constrain violence, and contribute to peace and security.

THE FUNCTIONALIST APPROACH

Directing attention away from putative and usually speculative origins of institutions and traditions, functionalists focused on the role a custom or practice played in the wider society of which it was part. This orientation grew out of a more intensive form of research involving lengthy residence in the communities being studied and communication by means of the local language. Ethnographic fieldwork of this type came to be labeled "participant observation."

Searching for the function of an institution meant looking for its consequences in other spheres. At least two different formulations were common: function as interrelationship with other cultural elements, and function as contribution to continuity and survival of the whole.

Radcliffe-Brown's demonstration of the connection between the informal and supportive relationships and the absence of formal authority, as between mothers' brothers and sisters' sons, on the one hand, and patrilineal descent organization, on the other, among the BaThonga and other groups, is an example of function as interdependence. So too is Nadel's illustration of the interconnection between witchcraft accusations and social relationships characterized by stress, conflict, and hostility, such as in the accusations by the cultivating husbands against their roving trader wives among the Nupe. Here function means concomitant variation, or co-variation, one phenomenon—practice, custom, behavior, belief, or activity—varying together with another one.

Examples of function as contribution to the cohesion, continuity, and survival of the wider society are seen in the other two examples discussed. Malinowski stresses the importance of initiation rituals in confirming tradition, ensuring conformity, and thus increasing social cohesion, all critical in tribal society. Gluckman points to cross-cutting ties and divided loyalties as defusing conflict and leading to a necessary level of peace and solidarity in society. Here function means the contribution to making society possible.

Chapter Three

Agency in Human Action
Social Processes and Transactions

In the village of Bisipara, in Orissa State, India, there was beginning in the early 1950s a long and ongoing conflict, recounted for us by F. G. Bailey (1957:ch. 11; 1969:116–21), between the "clean castes" of the priests, warriors, and herdsmen, and the ritually polluting "untouchable" Pan caste of landless agricultural laborers, music makers, beggars, and processors of dead animals. Pans were at the bottom of the social scale because of their polluting origins and occupations and were highly restricted by ritual constraints in their relationships with others. Traditionally they were also lowest in political standing and economic resources, Pan families being attached to and working for a family of warrior landowners in a permanent relationship called *raja-praja*, or king-subject.

However, during the first half of the twentieth century, many Pans had taken opportunities to improve themselves through education, government jobs, and the economic marketplace. By mid-century, many Pans were economically independent of the clean castes and relatively well to do. And the government had formally outlawed untouchability. But the Pans were unhappy with their continuing social position as low and despised. So they initiated a process of improving their social standing in the caste system (in principle impossible, in practice widespread if unacknowledged). First, on the symbolic front, they gave up various polluting practices, such as eating the meat of cattle, drinking alcohol, making music, and begging, and took on practices of clean castes, such as women dressing in long *saris* rather than short dresses, and men wearing the sacred thread, and building their own temple. Second, on the social front, they initiated a series of actions to gain recognition from the clean castes of their claimed, higher status. One of the actions was the following (Bailey 1969:118):

> The first incident which I witnessed in the conflict between the Pans and their fellow villagers took place at a [non-Pan] temple which lay about a hundred yards across open ground from where I lived. A procession of Pans, dressed in their best clothes, some carrying brass plates with offerings, and headed by a band of cymbal players and a man with a portable harmonium, came out of the village street and approached the temple. They do this every year, laying their offerings on the ground, from where the priest's assistant comes to take them into the temple. The clean castes . . . were coming meanwhile in ones and twos and taking their offerings into the temple antechamber. Shortly after the Pans reached the temple there was an altercation with the priest and his assistant: the Pans wanted to take their offerings into the temple claiming that under the Temple Entry Acts passed by the Orissa Government, they had the right to do so. The priest refused and sent a messenger for the headman, who lived fifty yards away. The headman came, accompanied by a large body of clean caste men. There was further quarreling, but in the end it died down and the Pans departed, back to their own street, without entering the temple. The clean castes left several young men standing guard around the temple, armed with battle-axes.

There were many further incidents, with the Pans often calling upon the police and judiciary in hopes of gaining external support for their claims.

SOCIAL EVENTS AS PROCESS

In this account of the conflict between the untouchable Pans and the clean castes, Bailey is emphasizing something different from the structure and function of early functionalist accounts (as described in ch. 2). Bailey, for the purposes of his account, takes for granted the hierarchical social structure of *varna* categories (priest, warrior, merchant, cultivator) and the endogamous *jati* caste groups; the *jajmani* system of customary economic division of labor and exchange; the Hindu religious concepts of *karma* (destiny), *dharma* (duty), and ritual purity and ritual pollution; and the functional interrelationship between the social structure and its economic roles and religious ideas. What Bailey focuses on is **social process**, the many acts of individuals through which the social structure is manifested. Beyond this, Bailey is emphasizing **strategic** processes through which some people hope to better themselves at the expense of others.

What some other authors have called social structure, Bailey (1969) refers to as **normative rules**, the set of conventional standards and regulations that determine what is correct and incorrect, what is right and what is wrong. These normative rules organize people and allocate benefits, whatever is valued in the society, such as social support, material wealth, status, power, and prestige. However, as Bailey shows, these benefits are also **prizes** in a competitive struggle among members of the society; and the **pragmatic** rules for winning this struggle are different from the normative rules. We see this in the case of the Bisipara Pans. Instead of accepting their conventionally understood, normative karma destiny and fulfilling their consequent dharma duty, they engaged in a strategic campaign, using both symbolic and social tactics, to raise their ritual status—although this is impossible according to the normative rules—and to thus increase their social prestige. This strategic campaign of the Pans, their attempted self-purification by rejecting polluting activities and by insisting on being accepted as equals, or at least clean, by conventionally higher castes, was one of many social processes that made up Bisipara village society and the life of Orissa State during the 1950s.

Bailey's (1969) book *Stratagems and Spoils: A Social Anthropology of Politics* is one of the works that brought to full maturity **processual theory** and analysis, an approach that had been developing among anthropologists, especially among British social anthropologists, throughout the 1940s and 1950s. Alongside continuing study of normative rules, social structures and institutions, and the functional relations amongst them, grew an interest in people's intentions, the options that they believed they had, the decisions they made, the consequent actions that they took, and the resultant actions of others. There was thus a shift away from thinking of people as acting strictly in terms of their statuses and roles, as if people always conformed to the normative rules. Rather, there was increased recognition that all people acted intentionally, that their intentions sometimes went beyond or outside of the normative rules, and that people's actions could change the structures and institutions within which they lived. This emphasis sees individuals in all societies and cultures as agents of their own actions and has more recently in anthropology been labeled **agency**.

TRIBAL CHIEFS UNDER COLONIAL RULE

In 1943, Isaac Schapera published *Tribal Innovators: Tswana Chiefs and Social Change 1795–1940* (as it was titled in its 1970 revision), a study of "legislative process . . . why those laws were enacted, and . . . how far they really succeeded in establishing new ways of life" (1970:v). In this work, Schapera (1970:vii) argues that "[s]ocial change in any one tribe was thus not determined rigorously by external influences and internal pressures alone; in part it depended also upon an unpredictable factor, namely, the kinds of persons its chiefs happened to be."

> The Administration imposed laws and sponsored developments which the Tswana were in effect obliged to accept. Chiefs also borrowed for their tribes various institutions and practices of European origin, and established others in direct response to European requests or advice. But they did not do indiscriminately whatever Europeans wanted of them; they sometimes modified or even rejected imported usages that they disliked. In addition, they made many changes that owed little or nothing to European influence, and some of which actually preceded the arrival of Europeans in Bechuanaland. They themselves thus contributed both substantially and independently to the transformation of Tswana life.

But it was not just the Administration and the Chiefs who had agency, the capability to act for the advance of their goals. So too did other Tswana tribesmen, as Schapera (1970:ch. 9) documents in a chapter called "Chiefs and Public Opinion":

> In the old days Tswana could apply various kinds of sanction against a chief of whose conduct they disapproved. His advisers were expected to warn or even reprimand him privately, and he might also be taken to task publicly at assemblies, where speakers did not hesitate to criticize him severely. If he failed to mend his ways, people would secede from him and go elsewhere, or a more popular relative would try to oust him by force, or, in the last resort, he might even be assassinated.

In other words, people did not just blindly follow their chief because they occupied the role of "subjects." Rather, they had definite ideas about what was good for them—which undoubtedly included a combination of normative and pragmatic rules, to use Bailey's terms—and expected that their chief would not stray too far from this, or else! That is, or else they would act on their own behalf, exercising their own agency, pursuing their own interests even at the expense of the interests of the chief.

LIVING AND SHAPING HISTORY IN NORTH AFRICA

Social process is not always at a micro-level, involving a few individuals in a village or a small group in a tribe. We see it also at the macro-level, involving large numbers of people; this macro social process is usually called "history." In it, many people are acting with definite intentions in mind, although they and many others often get swept up in their own and other people's actions. A remarkable report of macro social process came in 1949 from Evans-Pritchard, famous for his cultural study of witchcraft from the Azande (1937) and his social structural analysis of the Nuer (1940). In *The Sanusi of Cyrenaica*, Evans-Pritchard recounts a complex story involving the interplay of four distinct populations, set in Libya, North Africa.

One part of the story begins with pious and mystically inclined al-Sayyid Muhammad bin 'Ali al-Sanusi al-Khattabi al-Idrisi al-Hasani, who was born in Algeria around 1787 and pursued his Islamic religious studies in Algeria, then at Fez in Morocco, then traveled, preaching along the way, to Algeria, Libya, Egypt, and continued to Mecca and Medina in Arabia, studying and preaching and gathering disciples. In 1837, he founded a new mystical religious Sufi Order, the Sanusiya, of which he became the leader, the Grand Sanusi. As a result of political pressure, he left Arabia and returned to North Africa, eventually settling with his disciples in 1856 at the uninhabited, inland oasis at Jaghbub, 160 km south of the coast of Cyrenaica, the eastern portion of the Libyan coast. There the Grand Sanusi built the headquarters of the Sanusiya Order and used it as a base for missionary activity in all directions. He collected around him at Jaghbub a community of a thousand or so, many scholars, teachers, and students, who made good use of his library of some eight thousand volumes on Islamic law and jurisprudence, koranic exegesis, mysticism, philosophy, history, poetry, and astronomy and astrology. Jaghbub became an Islamic University of a high order of excellence, renowned for its poetry, and in Africa second only to al-Azhar University in Cairo (Evans-Pritchard 1949:ch. 1). This development of the Sanusiya Order resulted from the successful efforts of the Grand Sanusi in pursuing "the greater unity of Islam, his life's aim" (Evans-Pritchard 1949:11).

Two other parts of this story are the desert-dwelling Bedouin amongst whom the Sanusiya Order successfully proselytized and the Ottoman governors of Libya who occupied, on behalf of the Ottoman Empire centered in Turkey, the coastal towns and agricultural areas (Evans-Pritchard 1949:ch. 2). The Bedouin accepted the location of Sanusi lodges on their tribal and sectional borders and the mediation of disputes provided by the Sanusi Shaikhs resident in the lodges (Evans-Pritchard 1949:ch. 3). The Bedouin, occupied on a daily basis with raising camels, sheep, and goats, considered themselves warriors of God, ready to fight for the faith. But they were happy to have the members of the Sanusi Order pray and study in their stead and on their behalf. The Turkish Ottoman Administration (Evans-Pritchard 1949:ch. 4) formally recognized the Sanusi Order, and the Administration and the Order tolerated each other without liking each other. The Administration let the Order provide many administrative services for the Bedouin, but, with some help from the Order, continued to collect taxes, part of which had to be sent to Istanbul. Both the Ottoman administrators and the Bedouin tribesmen had their own interests, objectives, and priorities, as did the Sanusiya Shaikhs. There was continual negotiation among representatives among the three parties, notwithstanding the fairly stable understanding and arrangement among the three, an arrangement based upon the balance of intentions and capacities of the members of the three parties.

This delicate balance was broken by the entry of the fourth party, Italy. The Italian government wanted influence in and ideally control of Libya, which is not far to the south of Italy across the Mediterranean and was in past times an important province of the Roman Empire (Evans-Pritchard 1949:ch. 5). In fall 1911, having decided to invade Libya, Italy declared war on Turkey, bombarded coast towns, and landed troops to occupy them. Resistance was stiffer than expected, but the Turkish garrison retreated and withdrew to the interior. The Italians had expected the Bedouin to support the Italian invasion or at least stay neutral as the Bedouins' old Ottoman masters were driven out. But the Bedouin had other ideas, for the Turks "were quickly joined by contingents of all the Bedouin tribes of western Cyrenaica with the Shaikhs of the Sanusiya lodges at their head" (Evans-Pritchard 1949:109).

> Without these tribal reinforcements the Turks certainly could not have continued for long to resist. As it was, resistance not only became possible, but the whole character of the war changed, both in Cyrenaica and in Tripolitania [western Libya], where the Bedouin also flocked to the Turkish standards. It ceased to be a war in which a foreign power was trying to seize its colonies from a tired empire, and became a colonial war in the traditional sense of a European power attempting to deprive a native people of their liberty and their land. In Cyrenaica it became, in fact, more and more an Italo-Sanusi, rather than an Italo-Turkish, war and ended as a simple struggle of the Bedouin of Cyrenaica under Sanusiya leadership for freedom from a foreign yoke. (Evans-Pritchard 1949:110)

The war continued until 1917, when a truce accord was signed, but this was broken by the Italian fascist regime in 1923 and the second Italo-Sanusi war began. It continued, with "the Sanusiya emerg[ing] as an autonomous government with direction of its own armed forces, its own finances, and its own diplomacy," to the exclusion of Turkey, until 1932, when Italy defeated the Sanusiya-led Bedouin and chased the Sanusi leader, Sayyid Muhammad Idris, into exile in Egypt. Italy ruled and colonized Libya from 1932 to 1942, but during World War II was driven out of Libya by the British, with support from the Sanusi and the Bedouin. "Amid the roar of planes and guns the Bedouin learnt to see themselves more clearly as a single people, the Sanusi of Cyrenaica, in a wider world, and came to be regarded as such by those engaged in the struggle" (Evans-Pritchard 1949:229). At the end of the war, the

Sanusi leader, Sayyid Muhammad Idris, was crowned King Idris of Libya, and Libya became an independent state.

From a theoretical point of view, Evans-Pritchard's *Sanusi of Cyrenaica* can be seen as a processual study, primarily at the macro-historical level, with close attention to the purposes, intentions, choices, and actions of the people involved, in this case primarily collectivities rather than individuals. This work thus contrasts with Evans-Pritchard's earlier cultural study of the beliefs, values, and understandings of an African kingdom (1937) and his structural study of an African segmentary tribe (1940). In *The Sanusi of Cyrenaica* Evans-Pritchard demonstrates that an understanding of culture and structure alone are not sufficient for explaining human destinies; as well, we must take into account the agency and acts of the multiple parties and the events that these generate (see Salzman 1999, for my own discussion of this). Evans-Pritchard would continue with his structural studies (1951, 1971) and cultural studies (1956), suggesting that he saw structural, cultural, and processual approaches as complementary rather than distinct alternatives. At the same time, his commitment to processual analysis is clear in his general statement endorsing Maitland's position that "by and by anthropology will have the choice between being history and being nothing" (Evans-Pritchard 1962:26; originally presented in 1950).

ALLIANCES BETWEEN BLACKS AND WHITES IN SOUTH AFRICA

During the mid-1930s, Max Gluckman (1940, 1942) did research among the Zulu in South Africa. He summed up his analysis in one of his British Broadcasting Corporation radio lectures, published in *Custom and Conflict in Africa* (1959:ch. 6). Gluckman, himself by origin a South African (as was Schapera), was discussing modern South Africa, and the title of his discussion was "The Bonds in the Colour-Bar." Gluckman (1959:138–39) was addressing a basic question in sociology and anthropology: How can society exist?

> The divisions, the conflicts, the hatreds, between people and groups in South Africa are obvious enough. But how does the society keep going: wherein resides its cohesion? The striking problem here, as it was in feuding societies, is to show the order, not the quarrels, to see how quarrels are contained, not how they arise. . . . [W]hy does not South Africa explode?

Gluckman's (1959:139–40) answer is structural:

> Ultimately, of course, South Africa keeps going because the Whites wield superior force. . . . but it is not only the fear of this firepower

which keeps them working in a whole series of relationships with other colour-groups. I say, keeps them working—may I say, *kept* them working—because I am going to talk about conditions in the mid-thirties, when I was doing social anthropological research in one part of South Africa. I then came to the conclusion that it was money, as well as guns, which keeps South Africa going. Money does so by giving Whites and Blacks reciprocal, if also competing, **interests** in the whole economic system; and money introduces divisions in the ranks of each colour-group. Money is the prime factor, but there are, of course, also others which are important—education, religion, political alliances, even friendship. (Emphasis in italics in original; emphasis in bold added)

Zulu were led into military, administrative, and economic cooperation with Whites as some Zulu groups and individuals tried to gain advantage over other Zulu or simply tried to improve their own situations. For example, two Zulu sections went over to the British during the Zulu War. Some Zulu chiefs hostile to the Zulu king allied themselves with the Whites, as did some Zulu individuals alienated from their chiefs (Gluckman 1959:151). Others who looked for help from and established alliances with Whites included Zulu women trying to take control of their marriages away from male elders, younger Zulu sons who would not inherit the family herd, and ambitious Zulu individuals who saw improvement in education and government jobs. Zulu kings wanted armaments from Whites to fight their Black enemies. Many Zulu later desired peace and an administration that could guarantee it. Some Zulu, for example, farmers and livestock breeders, also wanted White technical assistance such as agricultural and veterinary services, and Zulu in all sectors wanted money and goods from the White sector. Thus, according to Gluckman (1959:151), "the system worked because from the beginning divisions of interest in the Zulu group led certain of its sections and individuals to seek alliances with certain White groups or individuals. . . . Sociologically, the principle might be stated as, 'divide and cohere'" (Gluckman 1959:164).

At the time that Gluckman was doing his research, Zulu had two types of officials over them: government commissioners and tribal chiefs. The government had the guns and thus the power, but the chiefs had traditional legitimacy. Zulus did not grant the government legitimacy, but they were prepared to operate within the political reality. Commissioners had to impose sometimes unpopular government measures but often offered services and opportunities. Chiefs stood for the Zulu against the government but were ineffectual in many areas and also sometimes made impositions on their tribesmen for their own benefit. Gluckman's (1959:159) analysis of this situation is processual, focusing on interests, calculations, options, and decisions of Zulu commoners:

> The Zulu were constantly comparing Black and White political officers and switching their allegiance according to what was to be

their own advantage, or by what values they were being guided on different occasions. This switching of allegiance was not a matter of attitude only, but of action. . . .

Of course, as Gluckman (1959:163) states clearly, while the society managed to operate through cross-cutting ties and conflicting allegiances, the problems of the Zulu could not really be solved by either commissioners or chiefs, or both together, within the unbalanced, race-based system of South Africa, which the Zulu considered oppressed them. Furthermore, as Gluckman predicted, the later imposition of *apartheid* divided Blacks and Whites in an even clearer fashion, and ultimately led, not to the parallel existence of racial groups as the inventors of apartheid hoped, but to the total breakdown of White-dominated South Africa.

PROCESSUAL ANALYSIS IN HISTORICAL PERSPECTIVE

Schapera's report on Tswana tribal chiefs and their followers, Evans-Pritchard's account of the Sanusi of Cyrenaica, and Gluckman's analysis of the Zulu in South Africa all illustrate that people are not passive conformists to "the rules" of society or social automatons mechanically fulfilling the "duties and obligations" of their "roles and statuses," but rather purposeful agents pursuing their own interests, as they define them, by considering the alternative possibilities, weighing and assessing their options, and choosing the course that seems most desirable. In other words, people act strategically, within the constraints of their situations, to bring about the results they desire to the maximum possible. Thus the social, economic, and political circumstances in which people live provide not only constraints, but also opportunities for pursuing goals or at least striving for the better over the worse. And so people do not just fit into social slots provided for them, but try to manipulate their social environment, and in so doing, not only affect their own lives and the lives of those around them, but also contribute to changes in the social arrangements and thus the cultural environment in which they live.

As an historical aside, it might be worth noting that critiques of structural functionalism formulated in the 1960s and 1970s (Asad 1973; Dahrendorf 1968; Harris 1968; Hymes 1969), and extended promiscuously to researchers identified as "functionalists," tended to be essentialistic, simplistic, and stereotypic. For example, commonly no distinction was made between structural functional heuristic theory, as set out in the works of Radcliffe-Brown (1952) or Malinowski ([1944] 1960), and the ethnographic analyses of researchers of the period (such as those reported here). Structural-functionalism was said to focus on the traditional culture of the natives rather than contemporary, colonial situations, to emphasize rules and norms of society rather than actual behavior, to limit research to static synchronic analyses that did not take change into account, and to assume normative, value consensus rather than recognize conflicts of interest and understanding, and overt social conflict. However appropriate these criticisms were in regard to functionalist heuristic theory, which in all frankness was not very elaborately developed, it would be quite mistaken to imagine that they could be fairly applied to "functionalist" researchers of the time, such as Schapera, Evans-Pritchard, and Gluckman, among others. These researchers, as we have seen in the cases described above, did focus on contemporary, colonial situations, on actual behavior, on change, and on conflicts of interest and overt social conflict. So the transition between "functionalist" anthropology and the processual and other anthropologies that came after was not as clear or abrupt as some critics have pretended.

In fact, none other than Radcliffe-Brown (1952:4), the main theorist of structural functionalism in anthropology, gave a very strong endorsement, in his final theoretical overview, to the study of process.

> My own view is that the concrete reality with which the social anthropologist is concerned in observation, description, comparison and classification, is not any sort of entity but a process, the process of social life. The unit of investigation is the social life of some particular region of the earth during a certain period of time. The process itself consists of an immense multitude of actions and interactions of human beings, acting as individuals or in combinations or groups.

Radcliffe-Brown (1952:4) furthermore explicitly directs attention to change:

> ... [W]hile we can regard the events of social life as constituting a process, there is over and above this the process of change in the form of social life. ... In comparative sociology we have to deal theoretically with the continuity of, and with changes in, forms of social life.

This orientation toward process and agency was endorsed and advanced by Raymond Firth (1964:ch. 2; article originally published in 1954), another important British social anthropologist, in an influential essay entitled "Social Organization and Social Change," through a conceptual distinction between social structure as general patterns in society and **social organization** as the actual processes of goal-oriented activities that are manifested in the exercise of choices by individuals.

SOCIAL PATTERNS AS PATTERNS OF CHOICES

Processual theory was advanced by Fredrik Barth's (1966) subtle and sophisticated formulations in *Models of Social Organization*. Barth's objective is to explain **social forms**. And his foundation argument is that "[t]o explain form one needs to discover and describe the processes that generate the form" (Barth 1966:v). Thus Barth (1966:v) labels his substantive, explanatory theories "**generative models**." As he (1966:1) puts it,

> My argument . . . is briefly summed up in the simple statement that our theoretical models should be designed to explain how the observable frequency patterns, or regularities, are generated.
>
> The most simple and general model available to us is one of an aggregate of people exercising *choice* while influenced by certain constraints and incentives. In such situations, statistical regularities are produced, yet there is no absolute compulsion or mechanical necessity connecting the determining factors with the resultant patterns; the connection depends on human dispositions to evaluate and anticipate. . . . This is also how we subjectively seem to experience our own social situation. Indeed, once one admits that what we empirically observe is not 'customs,' but 'cases' of human behaviour, it seems to me that we cannot escape the concept of choice in our analysis: our central problem becomes what are the constraints and incentives that canalize choices.

Barth (1966:1–2, 4–5), who quotes the Radcliffe-Brown passage set out above and refers favorably to Firth's discussion of social organization, is presenting his generative model as an alternative to another theoretical approach, one that characterizes society as a moral system made up of rules and norms, rights and obligations, to which people conform to a greater or lesser degree. The problem with this moral theory, according to Barth, is that it cannot explain who will and who will not conform, and why, and thus cannot explain actual behavior and the resultant social forms that we observe. In contrast, Barth (1966:2) argues, generative models can explain social reality:

> . . . [P]atterns of social form can be explained if we assume that they are the cumulative result of a number of separate choices and decisions made by people acting *vis-à-vis* one another. In other words, that the patterns are generated through processes of interaction and in their form reflect the constraints and incentives under which people act.

Let us take a simple example of a generative model from Barth's own work. In *Nomads of South Persia*, Barth describes the life of the Basseri tribe of pastoral nomads, tent dwellers who migrate up and down the Zagros Mountains with their sheep and goats. Within the wider region of Fars Province, these Basseri nomads appear to be a middle-class group, making a living working with their own livestock capital and supplying their own needs without great difficulty. They contrast with the rich, sedentary landowners of the upper class, who live luxuriously on the labor of others, and the poor, landless agricultural laborers, working for the landowners and receiving barely enough to live on, if not falling further and further into debt. Among the camping groups of the Basseri, which are the mobile residential communities, most families have from 80 to 150 sheep in their herds, and few if any have less than 80 and more than 200.

How can we explain this relatively narrow range of family herd size, remarkable in comparison with other pastoral groups in which family herds range from a few animals to thousands? Is there a rule among the Basseri that requires the restriction of family herds to the 80–200 range, to which group members must conform if they are to continue as members? Is there a rule, norm, or moral value to maintain middle-class status, or to maintain some degree of equality among fellow tribesmen? Not at all, says Barth; this pattern or "social form" is not the result of a rule. Basseri families would be permitted to stay in camps and migrate with a few animals or even none, or with many hundreds or even more.

Rather, this pattern, the restricted range of herd sizes, results from an aggregate, or totality, of choices made by Basseri as herd owners and managers of household economies. Here is how Barth ([1961] 1986:101–11) explains it. Sometimes through bad luck or bad management, Basseri household herds drop below sixty animals. This makes it virtually impossible to draw enough milk, wool, and lambs from the small number of animals in the herd to support a family. So the family has to draw directly on the capital, the productive animals themselves, either through direct consumption or (more likely) sale. But this reduces further the production of the ever smaller herd and requires even greater consumption of the capital. The result is a self-reinforcing downward spiral in animal numbers and production, and ends in the loss of the herd altogether. While the family could continue to migrate with their herding camp, it would have no way to feed itself, and the migrations would be pointless. In this situation, Basseri families drop out of herding camps and go to sedentary agricultural villages where work and some income can be found in agricultural labor. So no migrating Basseri pastoral families can be found with fewer than sixty animals, not because it would be wrong to have fewer than sixty animals, but because a Basseri family cannot be maintained on fewer than sixty animals.

Successful Basseri herders with large herds face other dilemmas. Their animals produce a considerable amount of wealth in dairy products, wool and hair, skins, and expendable male lambs and kids, as well as being worth a great deal themselves. However, there is a diminishing return on numbers of increased animals; that is, above a certain number the income per animal decreases. The problem is labor. When herds get beyond two hundred, family labor is not usually sufficient to deal with the flock. So nonfamily labor, whether hired hands or another family to take animals into their small herd, is required. And nonfamily labor, even when not purposely stealing products or abusing animals, does not take the same kind of care as does family labor. So even as the number of animals increases beyond several hundred, income increases at a much slower rate. At the same time, animal capital is highly volatile, being very vulnerable to disease, extreme weather, and predation such as rustling. Large herds can be lost very quickly. So for Basseri large herd owners, shifting their capital to a more stable form with a more reliable income is attractive. And there is such an opportunity, for flocks can be sold and agricultural land can be bought. This is exactly what most Basseri large herd owners do: become landowners and settle in villages, joining the landed gentry, and the lower ranks of the regional elite. As a result, there are no large family herds in Basseri herding camps.

As we have seen, among the Basseri, the nature of the families and family herds that make up camping groups is determined by which families stay and which families go. Barth's ([1961] 1986) analysis is a generative model because the pattern of herd sizes of the families making up the camping group is explained by the **strategic decisions** of some families to stay in the camp and the decisions of other families to leave the camp and settle in villages. To put it in Barth's terminology: the aggregate of decisions of Basseri herding families within the constraints and incentives of south Persian regional society, and the resulting pattern of selective sedentarization, lead to the "middle class" social form of the Basseri camp.

STRATEGIC TRANSACTIONS

Strategic decisions are also relevant to interpersonal relations; Barth (1966:3) argues that most (but not all [Barth 1966:4]) interpersonal relations are **transactional** in nature, requiring reciprocity between people. "In any social relationship we are involved in a flow and counterflow of prestations, of appropriate and valued goods and services." There is thus often a process of strategic evaluation in social relationships: ". . . parties in the course of their interactions systematically try to assure that the value gained for them is greater or equal to the value lost" (Barth 1966:4).

Put this way, one may see that transactions have a structure which permits analysis by means of a strategic model, as a game of strategy. They consist of a sequence of reciprocal prestations, which represent successive moves in the game. There must be a ledger kept of value gained and lost; and each successive action or move affects that ledger, changes the strategic situation, and thus canalizes subsequent choices. Many possible courses of action are ruled out because they are patently unsatisfactory, i.e. an actor must expect that value lost be greater than value gained. In such a model the incentives and constraints on choice are effective through the way they determine what can be gained and lost; and each actor's social adjustment to the other party in the transaction is depicted in terms of alter's possible moves, and how they in turn affect ego's value gains. The structure depicted in this model is a successional one over time—in other words, it is a model of process.

That is, relationships between people are commonly based upon an exchange of benefits, whether psychological, symbolic, or material. The exchange is subject to negotiation between people about what they expect. And a perceived imbalance in such an exchange can lead to renewed negotiation and, if not rectified, to breakdown of the relationship.

I think that we all, if we reflect, can recognize the place of reciprocity in our own relationships. Friendships, love relationships, and partnerships all entail expectations of mutually gratifying or useful exchanges. The anticipation of "unconditional" love, love demanding no return, is in most cases an example of the triumph of hope over experience. I recall a roommate with whom I shared an apartment when I was in graduate school. He was often calling on me, sometimes in the middle of the night, for help in his struggle with his psychological demons, and also found various ways that I could assist him in various practical tasks. But when I needed some help in one thing or another, he was always unavailable. It did not take me long to realize our friendship depended upon a highly imbalanced exchange: positive for him, negative for me. I finally terminated the relationship. And, as we all know, marriages these days often follow a similar course.

Barth (1966:5–11), however, is doing more than pointing to the importance of reciprocity in most social relationships; he is trying to explain the social form of complex relationships. He is pointing out that a focus on reciprocity can explain the way specific roles develop. Such sets of roles as friend/friend, husband/wife, graduate supervisor/graduate student, team captain/team member, and professor/professor are based on a foundation of a specific set of values and a set of status distinctions, which serve as generalized incentives and constraints, but the actual rights and obligations of the roles develop and take shape, over time, through negotiation over reciprocal exchanges.

Norms or rules develop, explicitly or implicitly, out of these negotiations that define those roles. As he (1966:9) puts it, "I would claim that we can observe the generative primacy of some factors, and the social processes of institutionalization; particularly, we can see how simple contracts about a few basic rights come first, and role stereotypes emerge afterwards." In other words, the norms of social roles and relationships are not established customs engraved in stone to which everyone has to conform. Rather, according to Barth, many of the expectations and rules in social relationships arise from strategic negotiation and transaction between actors. This transactional social process generates the detailed norms of social life. Barth is here arguing that social process is not just the manifestation of an established social structure, but precedes and generates social structure. In this processual theory, process is always going on and can reproduce social structure in the same form, or, if strategic decisions shift, can generate changes in social structure.

THE ORIGIN OF VALUES

If transactions between people depend upon the existence of a specific set of basic values, where do these values come from? Barth (1966:ch. 2) argues that we can understand the existence of generally established values in a culture through processual analysis. For when people interact and engage in exchange of goods and services, they need to have some common reference points of value in order to assess the offerings of one in relation to the offerings of the other. There is therefore among people engaged in transactions an ongoing process of constructing common values and scales of assessment through which different goods and services—whether political allegiance, provision of foodstuffs, sexual favors, provision of capital resources such as land or livestock or equipment, ritual services, biological reproduction, artistic production, and so forth—can be assessed in relation to one another.

> Whatever the basis for the transaction may be, through it the parties receive information indicative of each other's principles and scales of evaluation. Through repeated transactions I would argue that these aspects are reinforced, and that the values applying to those prestations which flow between parties become systematized and shared. They become systematized because when, and only when, we are faced with the repeated necessity of choice, are we forced to resolve dilemmas and make some kind of comparison between, and evaluation of, the alternatives with which we are presented. They become shared, or institutionalized, because in groping for a solution to the dilemmas, we prefer to use other people's experience as our guide rather than risk the errors implied in a trial-and-error procedure. Thus we adopt their principles of evaluation, and collectively grope towards a consistency of values. (Barth 1966:14)

Barth is here suggesting that the examination of process helps us explain not only human behavior and social forms, but also culture, or at least the consistency of values that is necessary for culture to be shared and held in common; his main point is that social transactions crystalize and generate consistency in values. Furthermore, when there are changes in the social context—such as new economic opportunities, or a new distribution of power—which influence the transactions, there is a feedback effect from the transactions to the values, which then are modified to reflect the new reality. "Thus actions can have a feed-back effect which make them logically on a par, and in a certain sense developmentally prior to, values and social arrangements" (Barth 1966:15).

Barth (1966:16) illustrates the "developmental primacy of action over institutionalized value" by describing (1966:18–19) what happened to Norwegian fishermen when they had the opportunity to switch from occasional, poorly paid labor on traditional ships to full-time, quasi-industrial, moderately paid labor on high-tech ships that would stay out for long periods. At first, the fishermen jumped at this new opportunity for full-time, better-paid work. But once they experienced it, they began to have second thoughts: What is the value of one's home life with one's family, of leisure time, of autonomy, and what is a fair wage for fishing that requires sacrificing these values? These fishermen had never before been faced with giving up these things, and so had not previously worked out their value in relation to paid work. The short-term result was considerable instability in the labor market, as crews just back from fishing quit en masse and had to be completely replaced by new crews. Future negotiations of contacts would include assessments of the value loss required by this new type of fishing and the pay required to compensate crew members. In this way, the process of transaction establishes the relative values of various activities in relation to one another, and a value framework is institutionalized that increases the commensurability, or integration in the culture.

Barth (1966:20) proposes that the distinction, widely accepted in anthropology, between social relations or interactions, on the one hand, and culture or values and beliefs, on the other hand, is a cause of theoretical difficulty, because social relations and culture are often incorrectly treated as separate and independent realms. In reality, Barth argues, we can see that transactions between people require both interaction and the formulation of value, so both social interaction and culture can be understood as part of a common process that generates the forms of social organization and the values. This means that social organization and values are not outside and independent of human actions, and human actions are not totally determined by the existing social organization and values, but rather that human actions are the source of organization and values. Consequently, and importantly, both social and cultural continuity and social and cultural change arise from human actions, particularly processes of decision making, transaction and exchange, and the formulation of encompassing value frameworks. From this processual point of view, social stability and continuity are not assumed, and cultural change is not mysterious but rather a result of aggregate shifts in human action.

For a further example of processual analysis of social change, let us return to Bailey's (1969:206–9) case of the Bisipara "untouchable" Pans and the Bisipara "clean castes." According to the normative rules that express cultural values, the Pans were ritually polluting and were excluded from many interactions with clean caste members, such as community leadership and decision making. According to the "traditional" pragmatic rules that express political and economic interest and advantage, the clean castes benefitted from excluding the Pans, keeping control entirely in their hands. This was the established situation before the Pans were able to take up educational and occupational opportunities provided by developments outside of the village.

Once some of the Pans were educated and held respectable jobs such as teachers, policemen, and businessmen, they were called upon by regional leaders to participate in the regional political system, and several had run as candidates in the Orissa State Legislative Assembly. So when members of the Bisipara village clean castes wanted something from the state government, such as a new school, it was in their pragmatic interest to call upon these Pans who had political standing in the state system to use their influence on behalf of the village. As these Pan leaders were repeatedly called upon by the village government, their inclusion began to be normal and even proper. Of course, these men were not included as Pans but as successful and influential men. The status of the Pans was, from the point of view of the clean castes, not open to negotiation or modification. The old normative rule of excluding Pans on the basis of ritual status was not openly challenged by the leaders of the clean castes. Rather, a new principle was enunciated, that achievement and capability should be the criteria for including individuals, and the rider, that caste would no longer be a criterion, remained unspoken.

In fact, a new normative rule, that leaders should be chosen on the basis of merit and influence, consistent with the new strategic choice of pragmatically including Pan leaders, supplanted the old, by that point pragmatically undesirable, normative rule of excluding Pans for ritual reasons. This change was obfuscated, by no one asserting that caste criteria were now less important, because caste remained important in other ways, and, if it had been made an explicit change of principle, clean caste villagers would have rushed to defend the caste principle and the old, now pragmatically undesirable, exclusion of Pans from village leadership. Often change is facilitated by obfuscation and the avoidance

of battles over general principles. While at the normative level the status of Pans had not changed, at the pragmatic level it had. Under such
circumstances as the pragmatic recognition of value, it is usual for the
normative status of such groups as the Pans to slowly improve and the
rationales for their lower status to be eventually discredited.

In this example as well as in others mentioned above, social forms
and cultural values are maintained or changed by the repeated decisions and transactions of aggregates of individuals. Continuity results
when people see it as their strategic interests to continue the same
choices and transactions as before; change results when people see it as
their strategic interest to make different choices and transactions than
they did previously. Normative rules and values are transformed or
replaced as patterns of choices and transactions shift. In processual
theory and analysis, societal institutions and cultural values do not
determine human action; rather, human action generates social institutions and cultural values.

Chapter Four

Determining Factors
Cultural Materialism and
Political Economy

Over 15 percent of the world's domestic cattle—199,300,000 head—are found in India, as compared, for example, with 10 percent of the world's total in Brazil and 8 percent in the United States (Galaty and Johnson 1990:8–9, Table 1.1). But the place that cattle have in Indian life is quite different from the place that cattle have in Brazil or the United States or elsewhere.

For the large majority of Indians who adhere to the Hindu religion, cattle are regarded as sacred, to be respected and revered according to the principle of *ahimsa*, the unity of life. The cow is a symbol of all life and is perceived and understood by Hindu Indians accordingly. The slaughter of a cow, or the eating of the meat of a cow, would be a gross violation of Hindu rules and would result in extreme **ritual pollution**. The "unutterable defilement" of such sacrilege, to use Harris's (1974:12) phrase, would be a violation of one's dharma, one's holy duty, and would transform, in a wholly negative fashion, one's karma, or destiny, particularly in future lives (in which beef eaters can expect to be reborn as cockroaches or other low forms of life). Furthermore, as **social status** in the **caste system** is tied to **ritual purity**, engaging in ritually polluting activities such as slaughtering cattle or eating beef would be a threat to the social standing of one's self, one's family, and one's *jati*, or subcaste group. For Indian Hindus, the cow is good to think but not good to eat. And, in fact, Indian cattle would not be very good to eat. They are undernourished, small, and skinny. Even in their huge numbers, they would not provide very much or very good beef.

For Americans North and South, the Indian cattle herd seems a bit pathetic. On the one hand, there are so many Indian cattle, but of such low quality and condition. On the other hand, there is so much potential nutrition going to waste in a land where poverty and hunger are still widespread. The ritual prohibition against both slaughtering cattle and eating beef seems highly irrational and profoundly unadaptive. Both Indian and foreign experts and commentators have criticized the condition and treatment of cattle in India as uneconomic and highly wasteful. How can we understand the Hindu belief in the sacredness of cattle and behavioral avoidance of slaughtering and eating cattle? Is it that Indians are much more spiritual than Americans, and that religion is such a powerful influence it overrides practical considerations and even the basic, biological needs of the people?

INDIA'S SACRED CATTLE ACCORDING TO CULTURAL MATERIALISM

In addressing this question, Marvin Harris (1966, 1974, 1979, 1994, and passim) argues that cultural beliefs, practices, and institutions that appear (to us) to be irrational and inscrutable—such as believing that cattle are holy, and banning the slaughter of cattle and the eating of beef—are best understood in terms of the material realities of people's lives, that is, in terms of the social, economic, and political systems in which they live. Human life and cultural practice, he argues, following Karl Marx, is rooted in the material world that feeds us, clothes us, and shelters us. Consequently, according to Harris (1979, 1994), cultural practices are best explained in terms of the way in which people make a living and reproduce themselves. This thesis he labels **cultural materialism**, and he characterizes it as a "research strategy"—in our terminology a "heuristic theory"—to guide the formulation of hypotheses and the collection of data or information to test the hypotheses.

Harris (1979:55), in specifying his core idea, quotes, referring to them as "a great advance in human knowledge," the famous words of Karl Marx:

> The mode of production in material life determines the general character of the social, political, and spiritual processes of life. It is not the consciousness of men that determines their existence, but on the contrary, their social existence determines their consciousness.

Harris elaborates by saying that the behaviors of people in economic production and biological reproduction tend to determine human behavior in family life and politics, and these tend to determine behavior and ideas in religion, philosophy, and other symbolic realms. This he calls "the principle of **infrastructural determinism**," that is, the **infrastructure** of production and reproduction determines the structure of domestic and political economy, and these determine the **super-structure** of symbols, myths, religion, and the like. For Harris, people's behavior always tends to determine their ideas. And in explaining cultural phenomena, the outside researcher's point of view, the **etic** perspective, always has precedence over the insider's, or participant's, point of view, the **emic** perspective. Harris (1979:58) justifies his heuristic theory of infrastructural determination by reference to the material basis of human existence:

> Thought changes nothing outside of the head unless it is accompanied by the movements of the body or its parts. It seems reasonable, therefore, to search for the beginnings of the causal chains affecting sociocultural evolution in the complex of energy-expending body activities that affect the balance between the size of each human population, the amount of energy devoted to production, and the supply of life-sustaining resources.

Harris thus tries to understand cultural beliefs and practices in terms of the underlying material (infrastructural) factors upon which people's lives and the continuity of the population depend.

What, then, of India's sacred cattle? Harris (1966, 1974; see also George 1990) argues that the belief in the sacredness of cattle and the prohibition of cattle slaughter and beef eating make sense in the context of Indian ecology and agrarian production. Harris points out that India's Zebu cattle are extremely important in Indian agricultural production: First, male-offspring bullocks pull the plows for the grain fields that produce 80 percent of the calories consumed by Indians. Second, in the wood-scarce Indian environment, cattle dung is the main fuel for cooking, without which grain is inedible. Third, cattle dung is a rich fertilizer that renews the agricultural land. Fourth, although buffalo are esteemed milk providers in India, Zebu cows provide around 50 percent of the milk for dairy products—a main source of protein and other nutrients—consumed by Indians. Fifth, the meat, skin, horns, and hoofs of dead cattle are consumed or utilized by the large population, probably 200 million, who are not "clean caste," that is, ritually pure, Hindus—the so-called untouchables and non-Hindus such as Muslims and Christians. Furthermore, the cost of supporting these highly serviceable cattle is virtually nothing, for they pasture on waste lands or consume agricultural waste products. The reason that the cattle appear to be in poor condition and unproductive is that they are maintained at little or no cost and provide a range of products and services rather than one form of production. A more accurate description of Indian cattle is that they are extremely hardy in difficult environmental conditions, highly versatile in the wide range of their contributions, and extremely low maintenance and cost. Indian cattle thus give much and take little. In terms of efficiency, calculated by dividing the useful calories produced by the calories consumed, Indian cattle are four times more efficient than American beef cattle raised on ranch land (Harris 1974:31).

If, as Harris says, Indian cattle are so efficient and play such an important part in agricultural production and the production of directly usable foodstuffs and materials, why is the use of cattle not just a business decision, and why are there beliefs that cattle are sacred and that it is horribly polluting to slaughter and eat cattle? Harris's (1974:21) answer is that what is rational for the individual and the short run, might not be viable for the individual in the long run or for the collectivity.

> During droughts and famines, farmers are severely tempted to kill or sell their livestock. Those who succumb to this temptation seal their doom, even if they survive the drought, for when the rains come, they will be unable to plow their fields. . . . Massive slaughter of cattle under the duress of famine constitutes a much greater threat to aggregate welfare than any likely miscalculation by particular farmers concerning the usefulness of their animals during normal times. It seems probable that the sense of unutterable profanity elicited by cow slaughter has its roots in the excruciating contradiction between immediate needs and long-run conditions of survival. Cow love with its sacred symbols and holy doctrines protects the farmer against calculations that are "rational" only in the short term.

So for Harris, the Indian belief in the sacredness of cattle is very important because it inhibits behavior directed to the individual and the short term, thus constraining behavior toward what is necessary—given the particular ecology and technology of India—for the population as a whole in the longer term. The importance of idea and belief systems, stated more generally, is that "the effective mobilization of all human action depends upon the acceptance of psychologically compelling creeds and doctrines" (Harris 1974:30; see also Harris 1979:72). Idea systems for Harris are thus a link in the causal chain that begins with ecological, demographic, and other material realities. Ideas do not determine the nature of a culture but are mental necessities if the system is to work.

KINDS OF INFORMATION AND EVIDENCE

Implicit in Harris's examination of sacred cattle in India are two analytic distinctions basic to cultural materialism. The first distinction (Harris 1979:32–33) is between emic and etic: emic refers to the insider's, or native's, understanding and point of view, while etic refers to the outside observer's point of view and understanding. The second distinction (Harris 1979:31) is between **behavioral** and **mental** processes: behavioral refers to body motions and their effects, while mental refers to our internal thoughts and feelings. Harris (1979:38) illustrates the four positions resulting from combining these two distinctions with an example from the sacred cattle discussion:

I   *Emic/Behavioral:* "No calves are starved to death."

II *Etic/Behavioral:* "Male calves are starved to death."

III *Emic/Mental:* "All calves have the right to life."

IV *Etic/Mental:* "Let the male calves starve to death when feed is scarce."

The insider's view of what is believed (III) is that all calves should live. The outside researcher's view of what is believed (IV) is that male calves can be allowed to starve in difficult times. The insider's view of what actually happens (I) is that no calves are starved. The outsider's view of what actually happens (II) is that some calves are starved.

For Harris, what people say to themselves and to others (III) may or may not reflect the principles on which they act or what an outside observer would infer that insiders think (IV). Similarly, what insiders say actually happens (I) may not be what an outside researcher observes (II). Cultural materialism encompasses all of these perspectives: emic and etic, and behavioral and mental. But there is an assumption that, ultimately, the etic perspective and behavioral processes will—as in the case of India's sacred cattle—explain and account for the emic perspective and mental processes.

In addition to the descriptive information (emic and etic, behavioral and mental) about cattle in India, Harris presents two additional kinds of analysis to support his case. One kind is **comparative**, as in showing the relative efficiency (mentioned earlier) of Indian cattle in relation to American beef cattle. Harris (1974:29) points out that within Hindu India the proportion of cows (which produce oxen and milk) to oxen (used for traction) varies. In dry districts, the ratio is seventy Zebu cows to one hundred oxen; in wet districts, where female water buffalo are the source of milk, the ratio drops to forty-seven Zebu cows to one hundred Zebu oxen. In other words, in wet areas Zebu cows are less needed, and, in spite of Hindu injunctions about the sacredness of the cow, people find a way to get rid of them. Harris thus shows that it is not religion, which is the same in both dry and wet districts, that determines how many cows you keep around, but ecology and how you get the food you need. Similarly, Harris (1974:29) compares wet and dry districts in Muslim Pakistan and Hindu India, and in spite of the absence of Hindu ideas of the sacredness of cattle and religiously motivated prohibitions on cow slaughter and beef eating, the overall ratio of cows to oxen is the same among Muslims and Hindus, sixty cows for every one hundred male animals. According to Harris, this shows once again that it is ecology and not religion that determines livestock practices. (Pakistanis must have other ideas that in extremity keep them from killing or selling their livestock, but Harris does not address this question.)

The other kind of analysis offered by Harris (1977:ch. 12; 1979:248–53) is **historical analysis**, in which different periods of history are compared and the reasons for transitions from one to the next are examined. (In a logical sense, historical analysis is a subcategory of comparative analysis, just as geographical or cross-cultural comparisons, e.g., wet vs. dry districts, and Hindu India vs. Muslim Pakistan, are other categories.) Archaeological evidence and ancient writings show that cattle were slaughtered and eaten in India from 4000 B.C. until A.D. 300. This use of cattle was particularly important for religious sacrifices and for honoring guests, who were called *goghna*, "one for whom a cow is killed." The Brahmin priestly class was in charge of sacrificing cattle and distributing the meat. But new and competing religious movements, Buddhism and Jainism, advocated ahimsa, the sacredness of all life, and the restriction or prohibition of slaughter and meat eating, and gained popularity. This doctrine was gradually adopted by the Hindu ruling and priestly classes. But why, and why at that particular moment?

In core regions of India, population had grown to many millions, great cities were built, and vast irrigation networks constructed. As agriculture spread and intensified, and forests were destroyed, droughts and famines became more frequent and more severe. People had to learn to live on less, and cattle became too costly, both environmentally and economically, to consume. The cow,

> an animal whose flesh was previously consumed became too costly to be used as food as a result of fundamental changes in the ecosystem and the mode of production. Its flesh therefore became the focus of a series of ritual restrictions. (Harris 1979:252)

In this analysis, Harris follows his basic principle of infrastructural determinism of structure (family, kinship, and politics) and superstructure (religion and ideology) in explaining beliefs and practices relating to cattle. He thus argues that changes in infrastructural factors—the environment (e.g., the expansion of agriculture and destruction of forests), population dynamics (e.g., increased population size and density), and production (e.g., the intensification of agriculture through irrigation)—have caused the changes in ideas about cattle and their proper uses, such as the transition from sacrificial slaughter of cattle and eating of beef to the prohibition of slaughter of cattle and the forbidding of eating of beef.

DIRTY SWINE AND EVIL WITCHES

Harris (1974:35–57) also develops a parallel case about cultural prescriptions and proscriptions in regard to pigs and pork. One of the cultural puzzles that he addresses is why cows came to be revered in India, while pigs came to be abominated in the Middle East. Just as in early times beef was eaten in India, pork was widely eaten in the Middle East from 7000 to 2000 B.C. During that period, there was a sixty-fold increase in human population and a corresponding rise in sheep and goat herds and in agriculture, resulting in deforestation. The decline of forested areas meant a decline in the natural habitat of pigs, which is shade and moisture, and in the natural diet of pigs, roots and nuts. As the natural environments of pigs disappeared, the cost of raising them increased, and pork became more and more of a luxury.

> The Middle East is the wrong place to raise pigs, but pork remains a succulent treat. People always find it difficult to resist such temptations on their own. Hence Jahweh was heard to say that swine were unclean, not only as food, but to the touch as well. Allah was heard to repeat the same message for the same reason: It was ecologically maladaptive to try to raise pigs in substantial numbers. Small-scale production would only increase the temptation. Better then, to interdict the consumption of pork entirely, and to concentrate on raising goats, sheep, and cattle. Pigs tasted good but it was too expensive to feed them and keep them cool. (Harris 1974:44)

Pigs were condemned as unclean, and even touching them was regarded as disgusting. Why in India were cows raised to holiness, while in the Middle East pigs were disparaged and abominated? The answer for Harris (1979:253) is once again ecology. In the Middle East, pigs could provide nothing but meat. With pork prohibited, pigs were useless, worse than useless, because they fed on grain and other crops meant for human consumption. A total ban was the ideal solution. In contrast, the Indian cow, even with beef prohibited, provided a multitude of valuable products and services to support Hindu cultivators. So it was for these, infrastructural reasons, that the pig became dirty and the cow became holy.

The prominence of ecology in Harris's explanation of Indian ideas about cows and Middle Eastern ideas about pigs does not mean that ecology is the main focus of cultural materialism. Ecology is the part or aspect of the infrastructure that is relevant in these cases. In other cases addressed by Harris, other aspects of the infrastructure, or of the structure, are identified as the main explanatory factors. Here are just two of the many cases discussed by Harris:

1. What lay behind the *potlatch*, the elaborate competitive feast (a ritual that can be considered part of the behavioral superstructure, in Harris's terms) among the Kwakiutl of the Northwest Coast of North America and other neighboring groups. This has been interpreted by some anthropologists, such as Benedict (1935), as a culturally induced striving for prestige (mental superstructure, in Harris's terms) by chiefs. In contrast, Harris (1974:111–30) argues that the potlatch is a manifestation of a **redistributive economy** (structure), which arises wherever population density and economic production (infrastructure) increase and adjacent communities have to establish relations (structure). Here Harris explains the ritual (behavioral superstructure) not in terms of culturally induced motivation (mental superstructure), but in terms of economic flows (structure) and productivity (infrastructure).

2. Another example is European witchcraft, or, to be more precise, the great wave of witchcraft trials and executions between the fifteenth and seventeenth centuries. This was a time of great social upheavals and uncertainty as rural, feudal society was being replaced by a more urbanized, manufacturing, mercantile society, and social relations became more impersonal and differences in wealth more apparent. All over Europe there were messianic movements supported by the peasants and urban poor, often taking a coercive or military form, which attempted to bring heaven on earth by getting rid of Church and state officials and distributing the wealth among all. The Holy Inquisition, a judicial enforcement arm of the Roman Catholic Church, received permission to root out not only heretics, who challenged the authority of the Church, but also witches, who were believed to be in league with the devil. By means of horrible and repeated tortures, people were made to confess, and then to name other witches. These measures generated an ever lengthening list of witches and a constantly elaborated dossier of outrageous if imaginary intercourse with the devil. During these centuries, some five hundred thousand people were burned as witches. Why did Church and state, not previously worried about witches, and hounded by heretical rebels, suddenly sponsor a self-expanding witch hunt? According to Harris (1974:207, 225–40), the witch hunt was the Church's defense against grass roots revolution. Witches served as a scapegoat to divert attention from complaints against Church and state by providing an alternative explanation of misfortune, and an imaginary and threatening, but in reality helpless, alleged adversary, against which the Church could act as an ally and savior of the people. Beliefs about

witchcraft (mental superstructure) and the campaign against alleged witches were thus generated by the class structure (behavioral structure) dividing the princes of the Church and state from the rural and urban poor, and by the political apparatus (behavioral structure) controlled by the elite.

In his formulation of cultural materialism, Harris has drawn on Karl Marx for his principle of infrastructural determinism. But Harris (1979:66–70) adds to Marx's focus on mode of production new emphasis on ecology and the environment, on demography and population, and reproduction. At the same time, Harris (1979:151–54, and ch. 6 passim) eschews as unscientific the Marxist **dialectic**, a formulation—often stated as "thesis/anti-thesis/synthesis"—drawn from Hegel that conceives of change as resulting from conflict (especially economic-class conflict), and then resolution (after the revolution). A research strategy, as far as Harris (1979:26) is concerned, must be scientific to be worth pursuing:

> The aim of scientific research strategies in general is to account for observable entities and events and their relationships by means of powerful, interrelated parsimonious theories subject to correction and improvement through empirical testing.

Cultural materialism is conceived by Harris as a scientific strategy directed toward explaining cultural phenomena:

> The aim of cultural materialism in particular is to account for the origin, maintenance, and change of the global inventory of sociocultural differences and similarities. (Harris 1979:27)

POLITICAL ECONOMY

If cultural materialism is a grandchild of Karl Marx, its close sibling is **political economy**. Perhaps I should say the "new" political economy is Marx's grandchild, for during the nineteenth century, when Marx was writing, "political economy" was an established discipline; it was the unified study of wealth, power, society, and culture. The development of the separate disciplines of economics, political science, sociology, and anthropology in the twentieth century split apart the old political economy. As far as Eric Wolf (1982:7–23) is concerned, research into human life and circumstances took a wrong turn when the disciplines divided and split up human reality, for they never could, never even tried, to put it back together into a coherent whole again. In the separate disciplines, the various aspects of human life—economy, politics, society, culture, and psychology—were examined independently and began being treated as things in themselves, with independent lives and self-determination. But in reality, according to Wolf, these are interrelated aspects of the human reality: There is no economy without politics, or culture without social relations, or psychology outside of the practical tasks and realities of life. Wolf turns back to political economy's

> concern with how wealth was generated in production, with the role of classes in the genesis of wealth, and with the role of the state in relation to the different classes (Wolf 1982:20).

The focus on production is not, however, on a narrow aspect of human activity, for, according to Wolf (1982:21), Marx's conception of production was very broadly conceived:

> For him, production embraced at once the changing relations of mankind to nature, the social relations into which humans enter in the course of transforming nature, and the consequent transformations of human symbolic capability. The concept is thus not merely economic in the strict sense but also ecological, social, political, and social-psychological. (Wolf 1982:21)

In this spirit, Wolf (1982:23) focuses his conception of political economy of culture and society on "**material relations**," that is, people interacting with nature in the course of production, interacting with one another in relations of production that differentiate them into classes, and interacting with centers of power that use coercive force to shape production and social relations.

Furthermore, Wolf (1982:3–19) argues, this political economy perspective guides us to see beyond the artificial confines of reified societies and cultures and to treat them not as totally separate worlds but rather as specific loci of regional and international flows of people, goods, influence, and power. In other words, understanding particular local or regional societies and cultures, and their social patterns, beliefs, and customs, requires seeing them as part of wider political and economic fields in which there are forces that influence and shape those societies and cultures. (These are ideas also developed by Andre Gunder Frank [1966] and Emanuel Wallerstein [1974], whom Wolf [1982:22] acknowledges.) So anthropologists studying Sicilian villages, for example, have to be aware that community society and culture have been shaped by government political and economic policies in Naples and Rome, by national and international politics, and by the international markets for grain and other commodities (as shown in two political economy studies: Blok 1974 and Schneider and Schneider 1976). In this way, political economy as a heuristic theory forces anthropologists to remove the narrowing conceptual blinders of "culture" and "society" to see the regional and international, **transcultural** flows and forces that influence the shape of local social and cultural life. According to this view, particular cultural values and beliefs or social organization and institutions can no longer be attributed to inherent cultural patterns or to the functional interdependence of social institutions. Rather, people's ideas and relations must be seen as responses to the broader regional and international field of economic and political forces within which they must live and make a living.

EXPLAINING TRIBES

To illustrate, let us return (continuing our discussion from chapter 3) to the Basseri tribe of pastoral nomads described by Barth in *Nomads of South Persia*. The Basseri tribe, and many of its neighboring tribes in the Zagros Mountains, such as the tribes of the Qashqai confederation (Beck 1986), have strong chiefs, *khan*, and sometimes strong confederacy chiefs, *il-khan*. Among the Basseri, the chiefship is the "pivotal position" of the entire tribal organization:

> The scattered and constantly shifting tent camps of the Basseri are held together and welded into a unit by their centralized political system, culminating in the single office of the chief. (Barth [1961] 1986:71)

The chief is "the central, autocratic leader of the tribe . . . [P]ower is conceived as emanating *from* him, rather than delegated *to* him by his subjects" (Barth [1961] 1986:71–72, emphasis in original). This means that the chief has "power of decision and autocratic command over his subjects" (p. 74). But this right to command "is a strictly chiefly prerogative," no other role or individual in the Basseri having it.

> The fields in which the chief regularly exercises authority, i.e. his main functions for the tribe, may be grouped in three: allotting pastures and co-ordinating the migrations of the tribe; settling the disputes that are brought to him; and representing the tribe or any of its members in politically important dealing with sedentary authorities. (Barth [1961] 1986:76)

The chief and his extended family (including uncles, brothers, nephews, and their families) make up an elite, ruling class, distinct from ordinary tribesmen. Most ordinary tribesmen live in modest tents, own small herds, and spend their days husbanding their herds and otherwise making a living in the countryside. In contrast, the chief and his family members usually have luxurious villas in Shiraz, the provincial capital, as well as spacious and elaborate tents in the countryside, large herds, and many luxury animals such as horses and hawks. As well, members of chiefly families are often landowners; it is usual to hear that they own several villages. Tribal chiefs and their families commonly spend their time as much in town with sedentary members of the urban and regional elites as out in the country looking after their interests or meeting with tribesmen. Chiefs and their families are supported not only by their own property, but by taxes from their tribesmen. The Basseri chief has the right to ask for one, two, or three sheep per hundred from his tribesmen, which would amount to thousands of sheep (Barth [1961] 1986:74). The 3,000 tents of Basseri families (p. 1), with an average of around 80 sheep per tent (p. 17), gives a total of 240,000 sheep. If the chief asks for 1 in 100, he gets a total of 2,400 sheep; if he asks for 3 of 100, he gets 7,200 sheep. At a per sheep cash value of 80 *toman*, the 7,200 sheep in tax income are worth 576,000 toman, an amount that would cover the expenditures of more than 100 families of ordinary Basseri tribesmen at 5,000 toman for a whole year.

This picture of the Basseri tribe, with its centralized and autocratic authority, and its hierarchical class division, is strikingly different from accounts of acephalous (headless), decentralized, egalitarian, nomadic tribes such as the Nuer of the Sudan (Evans-Pritchard 1940), the Somali of the Horn of Africa (Lewis 1961), and the Yomut Turkmen of Central Asia (Irons 1975). These acephalous tribesmen live in what Evans-Pritchard has famously called "ordered anarchy," and are, as the famous explorer Richard Burton (cited by Lewis 1961) put it for the Somali, "a fierce and turbulent race of Republicans." These tribes have no chiefs and no economic classes; to the extent that there are leaders, they are primarily mediators and depend heavily on public opinion. In decision making, independence and autonomy of the individual, rather than authority, are stressed. Within the general strictures of the cultures, people are free to act according to their own lights, and they defend their individual liberty and autonomy tenaciously.

How can we account for the differences between the centralized, hierarchical Basseri and the decentralized, egalitarian nomadic tribes? Is there an inherent, cultural tendency for Persians such as the Basseri to seek strong leaders (as some commentators have suggested), while these other cultures have an inbuilt value favoring resistance to hierarchy and domination? Some doubt is shed on this hypothesis by the comparison of the Turkic Qashqai neighbors of the Basseri, with the Turkic Turkmen of Central Asia, for the Qashqai are, like the Basseri, highly hierarchical, while the equally Turkic Turkmen are extremely egalitarian and decentralized. Perhaps, then, the difference is to be explained, as Wolf and the political economists suggest, by different economic and political environments and differential relations with powerful influences in that broader field.

Barth ([1961] 1986:77) makes clear that the structure of the Basseri chiefship is closely tied to relations with outsiders:

> Perhaps the chief's most important function is to represent the tribe in its relations with the Iranian administration, and in conflicts with sedentary communities or persons. . . . Where persons or groups belonging to such different parts of a plural society meet, there must be mechanisms mediating the relationship between them. . . .

In other words, the Basseri chief is there to deal with the Shah of Iran and his officials and army, the businessmen of the urban bazaars, the agriculturalists of the villages, and the other, neighboring tribes. Basseri tribesmen do not need a chief so much for internal matters, as to deal with outside forces that have a great influence on them. Therefore, as the political economists would say, the culture and organization of the Basseri tribe is decisively shaped by the wider field of economic and political forces in which it exists, these forces being the Iranian state that claims ultimate authority over them, the marketplace upon which they depend to buy and sell, the agriculturalists with whom they trade, and the other tribes with whom they must share pastures. One way in which the Basseri deal with outsiders is by presenting an image of themselves as a strongly unified and disciplined group under a powerful and authoritarian chief, although in reality the chief must defer to public opinion among his tribesmen (Salzman 2000a).

What, then, explains the nature of the acephalous, egalitarian tribes? The answer is that their political and economic environments were much less dense than the Basseri's: The Nuer and the Somali did not have an effective state presence to deal with; they were sovereign in their own lands. They were also economically self-sufficient, producing for their own consumption and involved in little or no trade. They did not live amongst other populations, making mediation unnecessary. And their population density was low, reducing both the possibility and necessity of centralized coordination. The Yomut Turkmen also had a low population density, but had a somewhat more dense political-economic environment than the Nuer and Somali. They were on the margins of the Iranian state but maintained their independence from it by military might and by easy escape deeper into Central Asia. They did frequent the distant markets of Central Asia to sell carpets and captured Persians as slaves. And nearby Persian populations were either extorted for protection money or raided for slaves. So the Turkmen dealt with the other occupants of their wider area through fight or flight, extortion or extraction; they needed no chiefs for mediation with outsiders—their rifles and horses sufficed. The Yomut Turkmen remained egalitarian and decentralized, and they mobilized, when necessary, through their corporate lineages, as did the Nuer and Somali.

Yet other cases, tribes with leadership roles, but relatively weak ones, such as the Yarahmadzai Baluch (Salzman 1983, 2000b) and the Rwala Bedouin (Lancaster [1981] 1997), intermediate in political structure between the hierarchical Basseri and the egalitarian Nuer, Somali, and Turkmen, had political and economic environments denser than the egalitarian tribes but less dense than the hierarchical ones. The Yarahmadzai Baluch were in the immediate vicinity of a powerful Kurdish *hakomate*, a small feudal society, and, repeatedly in negotiations with it, needed a spokesman to represent them. Once the Yarahmadzai were conquered by the Persians, in 1935, their chief, *sardar*, became the middleman between the tribe and the state, and the chief became stronger and the tribe more hierarchical than in the past. The Rwala Bedouin, though spread across the northern Arabian desert and able to move across borders between Saudi Arabia, Jordan, and Syria, did have ongoing dealings with governments and markets. Their *sheikhs* acted as intermediaries between the tribe and external agencies, but they were not so much rulers as middlemen, able to act only to the extent that they represented public opinion. No Rwala was obliged to obey a sheikh, and each Rwala had the freedom and responsibility to decide and act on his own.

This analysis of the reasons for the strong chiefship among the Basseri, Qashqai and other Zagros tribes, the weak leaders among the Baluchi and Bedouin tribes, and the acephalous organization among the Nuer, Somali, and Turkmen, supports the position of the political economists that the nature of people's social relations and ideas is strongly affected by the wider political and economic environments in which they live, and that no tribe or community or population can be understood as an entity on its own, without considering its broader social environment.

MODES OF PRODUCTION

Wolf (1982:ch. 3) and other political economists go beyond the general directive that people, societies, and cultures must be understood in terms of the wider political and economic fields in which they are immersed, by arguing that some factors in those fields are more influential than others. Their position is that, because people are part of nature and must draw their living from nature, and are social beings who make their livings socially, this **material basis** for human life and social life is the primary influence of people's lives and destinies. The term "**production**" represents for political economists the complex of natural resources, labor, and organization that they argue is the foundation of society and culture. Ideas, beliefs, and values reflect the material realities of production (Wolf 1982:75). This formulation, drawn from Karl Marx, is close to Harris's principle of infrastructural determinism.

The different ways in which nature, labor, and organization are related are different **modes of production**, and each mode has a different way of affecting the lives and life chances of the people involved. A mode of production is

> a specific, historically occurring set of social relations through which labor is deployed to wrest energy from nature by means of tools, skills, organization, and knowledge. (Wolf 1982:75)

Wolf (1982:76–99) defines three main modes of production: a kin-ordered mode, a tributary mode, and a capitalist mode.

1. In the **kin-ordered mode of production**, ideas about kinship ties define social relationships that are used to draw on nature in making a living (Wolf 1982:91). How this works out in practice depends upon whether natural resources are available to anyone, or only to those with specific social ties. Where resources are open to everyone, kinship is used to build flexible bands and networks of relations between bands; where resources are restricted, kinship group membership is used to give members access and exclude outsiders.

2. In the **tributary mode of production**, power and domination—political processes—are used to organize production, including the mobilization of labor and transformation of nature. A powerful ruling elite, either local or regional, extracts surplus for its own consumption by controlling strategic resources such as land, irrigation systems, or trade, and also by controlling the means of coercion, such as the army. Where local elites are in control, there are systems sometimes called "feudalism"; where regional elites are in control, the system is sometimes labeled "despotism."

3. In the **capitalist mode of production**, the means of production are monopolized by those with monetary wealth, and those without access to the means of production must sell their labor to make a living. Furthermore, the owners of the means of production keep the products that their labor force produces, and sell those products for more than the cost of the labor to their laborers and others, retaining the profits from those sales. True capitalism develops when some of the profits are reinvested in production to increase and expand production and profits.

TAPPERS AND TRAPPERS

The predominance of production can be seen in the transformations of society and culture as people are drawn away from one form of production and into another. Many of Wolf's (1982) cases follow this pattern, including discussions of North American fur trappers and South American rubber tappers (1982:158–94, 326–30). The Mundurucu of the Amazon Basin in Brazil (Murphy and Steward 1956; Wolf 1982:326–29) came into contact with Europeans around 1800. They lived in autonomous villages but cooperated and married between villages.

Organized into patrilineal clans and residing patrilocally, with wives coming from other villages to live with their husbands, they made their living through men's hunting and fishing and women's slash-and-burn horticulture. During the first two thirds of the nineteenth century, the Mundurucu were drawn into commercial trade, the Europeans providing manufactured trading goods such as steel tools, firearms, cloth, and utensils, and the Mundurucu providing manioc flour. The increased importance of horticulture, carried out collectively by groups of related women, led to a change in residence pattern, from patrilocal to matrilocal, so that men came to live in their wife's village. Thus men from different villages and clans found themselves living in the same village. In the latter part of the nineteenth century, trade in rubber, drawn from wild rubber trees that grew along the rivers, became very important. Men decreased hunting to spend more time tapping latex from the trees, and they became more dependent on food from trade for subsistence. Traditional tribal chiefs, representing the village in trade, fell under the control of the traders and were eventually replaced by chiefs, "captains," appointed by the traders. Traditional leadership was thus undermined and eventually collapsed, with each rubber collector dealing directly with the trader. And then the entire community structure collapsed, as the tappers, now spending the greater part of their year among far-flung and dispersed wild rubber trees, finally moved their households to their tapping areas, resulting in the replacement of village residence by widely dispersed, single-household homesteads.

Among many northern, North American, aboriginal hunting peoples, engagement with the fur trade transformed their production activities, consumption patterns, organization, and culture (Murphy and Steward 1956; Wolf 1982:158–94; cp. Bishop and Morantz 1986). Northern peoples, such as the Algonkians, living in small, flexible, nomadic hunting bands, began to trap beaver in exchange for manufactured trade goods from Europeans. At first the trapping was a sideline, with hunting the main source of foodstuffs and other subsistence needs. But with the influx of more consumer goods, people shifted to full-time trapping, thus becoming more dependent upon trade goods for food. It was increasingly unnecessary to live out in the hunting grounds, and increasingly arduous to cart trade goods out to the bush, so trappers began to leave their families at the trading post, which became the focus of residence. At first, trapping, like hunting, was done in groups, the catch was shared, and everyone was free to trap where they chose. But this was soon replaced by private traplines and individualized trapping territories. Residential groups became larger as they consolidated around trading posts, and formal leaders, never known before, were appointed to deal with the traders. But at the same time, production became an activity and ownership the right of the individual family, thus undermining the collective arrangements of the past. In some places, individuals began claiming exclusive ownership of trapping areas, even against their immediate family members.

Although the tropical forest tappers and the northern trappers had very different aboriginal cultures and forms of organization, their transformations in response to the common influence of commercial trading show remarkable parallels. Murphy and Steward (1956) formulate a generalization about the initial change:

> When goods manufactured by the industrialized nations with modern techniques become available through trade to aboriginal populations, the native people increasingly give up their home-crafts in order to devote their efforts to producing specialized cash crops or other trade items in order to obtain more of the industrially made articles.

That this change has major effects on the local culture is obvious from the two cases discussed. Murphy and Steward (1956) also frame this as a generalization:

> When the people of an unstratified native society barter wild products found in extensive distribution and obtained through individual effort, the structure of the native culture will be destroyed, and the final culmination will be a culture-type characterized by individual families having delimited rights to marketable resources and linked to the larger nation through trading centers.

For materialist theorists in general and political economists in particular, the processes of transformation described here illustrate not only the impact of forces from the wider world, but also the dominance of production over other aspects of culture. The Mundurucu shift from horticulture for subsistence to expanded horticulture for trade led to a change from a patrilocal to a matrilocal residence pattern, and the later replacement of hunting for subsistence by rubber tapping for exchange led to breakdown in the village political and social organization and the emergence of the individual family as the residential and economic unit. The Algonkian shift from subsistence hunting to commercial trapping led to a switch from small nomadic bands to larger, stable villages centered on trading posts, and a switch from collective hunting and sharing to individualized control of trapping territories and family economic units.

As these examples show, materialist theorists attempt to explain social and cultural patterns by identifying the particular material conditions that underlie them. Materialist analysis is commonly framed as scientific, historical, or both, and materialist theory posits an objective truth to be discovered. At the same time, however, there is in materialist approaches a parallel moral dimension manifested in the concern, sympathy, and advocacy for the downtrodden, oppressed, and exploited.

This is evident in the work of Karl Marx and his advocacy for the "workers of the world," and in the work of Harris and Wolf for those who have suffered as a result of the power of others. Materialist analysis, in this moral sense of advocacy, can be understood as a kind of intellectual **deconstruction** of social arrangements and cultural understandings to expose and thus debunk exploitation and oppression.

Chapter Five

Coherence in Culture
Dominant Patterns and
Underlying Structures

> The Zuni are a ceremonious people, a people who value sobriety and
> inoffensiveness above all other virtues. Their interest is centered
> upon their rich and complex ceremonial life. Their cults of the
> masked gods, of healing, of the sun, of the sacred fetishes, of war,
> of the dead, are formal and established bodies of ritual with priestly
> officials and calendric observances. No field of activity competes
> with ritual for foremost place in their attention. Probably most
> grown men among the western Pueblos give to it the greater part of
> their waking life.

So Ruth Benedict ([1935] 1961:42–43) in *Patterns of Culture* characterizes the Zuni of the Pueblo culture of New Mexico. For Benedict, the
Pueblo peoples, including the Acoma and Hopi as well as the Zuni,
illustrate a particular type of culture in which order, moderation, tradition, and collectivity are the standards that define goodness: the
Pueblo are people "all of whose delight is in formality and whose way
of life is the way of measure and of sobriety" (Benedict [1935] 1961:93).
Benedict, drawing on the philosopher Friedrich Nietzsche's thought,
labels this moderate and formal way of life "Apollonian," after Apollo,
the ancient Greek sun god.

> Zuni ideals and institutions . . . are rigorous . . . The known map,
> the middle of the road, to any Apollonian is embodied in the com-
> mon tradition of his people. To stay always within it is to commit
> himself to precedent, to tradition. Therefore those influences that
> are powerful against tradition are uncongenial and minimized in
> their institutions, and the greatest of these is individualism. (Bene-
> dict [1935] 1961:57)

Among the Pueblos, the individual must act only as part of a collectivity, and only according to the established routines and formal procedures.

> Just as according to the Zuni ideal a man sinks his activities in those of the group and claims no personal authority, so also he is never violent. Their Apollonian commitment to the mean in the Greek sense is never clearer than in their cultural handling of the emotions. Whether it is anger or love or jealousy or grief, moderation is the first virtue. (Benedict [1935]1961:76)

The ideal Zuni man is mild, pleasant, agreeable, yielding, and generous. He would never express strong emotions or seek power or authority (Benedict [1935] 1961:71), and wishes only to play his proper part in the established tradition of the pueblo.

Apollonian Pueblo culture is contrasted by Benedict ([1935] 1961:56 and passim ch. 4), following Nietzsche, with the Dionysian cultures of other North American native peoples. Called after Dionysus, the ancient Greek god of wine, Dionysian cultures look not to daily life but to soaring beyond it, not to a calm and methodical repetition of rituals but to extreme emotional states of ecstasy, not to the established norms of the collectivity but to the imaginative insights of the individual, not to the authority of tradition but to the power of the striving, superior individual. While the Apollonian people of the Pueblo culture valued calmness and mildness, eschewing strong emotions, the native Dionysian cultures of North America sought every means to reach ecstatic experience, including customary use of pain resulting from self-torture and extreme conditions, of intoxication from alcohol and drugs, and of metabolic imbalance through fasting. By these means, individuals sought the vision-dream that was associated in their minds with supernatural power. In politics and warfare too, individualism and extreme exertion were the model; ambitious individuals imposed their leadership through their strength, just as sorcerers killed the weaker to increase their strength, and warriors counted coup by audacious feats of bravery against the enemy. Initiation into adulthood was brutal, and mourning was agonized in the Dionysian cultures, while in the Apollonian Pueblo culture initiation was gentle and mourning was constrained. The contrast between the mild, formal, and sober Pueblo Apollonians and the assertive, striving, self-intoxicating Dionysians of native North America could hardly be more marked.

CULTURE PATTERNS AND CONFIGURATIONS

For Benedict, there are several important general understandings that are illustrated by this case (and others that she analyzes along the same lines). The first (Benedict [1935] 1961:17 and passim ch. 2) is that different cultures are based upon different principles and have different emphases and values.

> In culture . . . we must imagine a great arc on which are ranged the possible interests provided either by the human age-cycle or by the environment or by man's various activities. . . . [A culture's] identity as a culture depends upon the selection of some segments of this arc. Every human society everywhere has made such selection in its cultural institutions. Each from the point of view of another ignores fundamentals and exploits irrelevancies. One culture hardly recognizes monetary values; another has made them fundamental in every field of behaviour. In one society technology is unbelievably slighted even in those aspects of life which seem necessary to ensure survival; in another, equally simple, technological achievements are complex and fitted with admirable nicety to the situation. One builds an enormous cultural superstructure upon adolescence, one upon death, one upon after-life.

Each culture draws upon and is organized around certain aspects of human life, and deemphasizes or ignores various other aspects of human life. Each culture asserts certain values to the exclusion of others.

The second general principle, which follows from this diversity seen across human cultures, is that it is inappropriate and uninformative to explain or evaluate one culture by the perspectives and values of a different one. A culture can be understood only in terms of its own values and perspectives. To evaluate Apollonian Pueblo culture by the values and criteria of Dionysian Plains culture, or Plains culture by the norms of Pueblo culture, would be no more than an exercise in ethnocentrism. Rather, Benedict ([1935] 1961:26) guides us toward **cultural relativism**, which as an approach to research means that a culture must be understood in its own terms, according to its own presuppositions, rather than by criteria and values from another culture. She urges tolerance toward cultural divergences, and the appreciation that other people's cultures are meaningful to them in the same way that our culture is to us.

Benedict's ([1935] 1961:ch. 3) third general understanding is that a culture is not just a collection of various customs, norms, institutions, values, and practices that have been selected from the range of human possibilities. Rather, each culture is integrated into a whole that tends toward consistency. All aspects of behavior and of organization are "made over into consistent patterns in accordance with unconscious cannons of choice that develop within the culture" (Benedict [1935] 1961:34). This is why looking at individual customs or practices is insufficient; it is their place in the whole and their integration into the overall **configuration** that defines their significance. We can see here the influence on Benedict ([1935] 1961:36) of *Gestalt* (configuration)

psychology, which argued that human perception grasps overall patterns rather than a multitude of details. Benedict ([1935] 1961:31)
argues that "adequate social orders can be built indiscriminately upon
a great variety of these foundations," and that any institution or
emphasis that serves as the dominant one in a culture has been developed far beyond its original purpose. In other words, the crystallization
of a culture pattern is not a necessary result of circumstances, but
rather is a creative formulation of the human imagination. Benedict's
theory can justly be called **configurationalism**.

Benedict, however, did not imagine that a culture is invented in
isolation and in totality, generating the elements of its configuration
with no external influences. She was a student of Franz Boas (who, by
the way, contributed the introduction to *Patterns of Culture*) and appreciated the historical influences on each culture and the extent to which
each culture drew on materials borrowed from others. (The theory
emphasizing cultural borrowing is called **diffusionism** [see, e.g., Kroeber 1948] and has sometimes been presented as an alternative to **evolutionism**.) But Benedict's insight, and this is her fourth general principle, is that cultures select elements from their environment according
to their suitability for the established configuration, and that elements
selected, or imposed by unavoidable external pressure, are interpreted,
construed, and transformed so that they are consistent with existing
cultural elements and concordant with the overall configuration, the
dominant pattern of the culture (see **cultural selection**). Benedict
([1935] 1961:ch. 4) illustrates this point with examples from Pueblo culture. Although neighboring cultures used torture, drugs, and alcohol,
the Pueblo peoples rejected these practices entirely. And while the
Pueblo peoples did incorporate fasting and dancing into their cultures,
fasting and dancing were never used in Pueblo to intensify emotion,
bring on frenzy, and induce visions; fasting was used only to purify
before ceremonials (Benedict [1935] 1961:63) and dancing was always
monotonous and orderly (p. 66). Similarly, initiation rituals that in sur-
rounding cultures were brutal ordeals, were in Pueblo gentle and mild
(p. 74). So cultures maintain their forms as new and external elements
are selected and reshaped according to the cultures' particular orientations and emphases.

Benedict's formulation of "patterns of culture," of "cultural configurations," is an attempt to explicate the nature and substance of cultures, rather than to explain cultures in a causal sense. Benedict's concepts are meant to help us understand each culture in its own terms.
She offers no causal theory about the reason for the particular configurations of specific cultures, no explanation of why the Pueblo cultures
took up an Apollonian approach while others took up a Dionysian
approach. Benedict's goal is to describe more sensitively and insight-
fully the specific cultures of particular peoples. She ([1935] 1961:27)

rejects "the temptation to generalize into a sociological law . . ." and emphasizes ([1935] 1961:14) the need to "understand the immensely important role of culturally conditioned behaviour."

Ruth Benedict and Margaret Mead were both students of Franz Boas at Columbia University and were friends and collaborators. They influenced one another and together contributed to this configuration-alist theoretical vision. The participation of the individual psyche in the configuration of culture, and the shaping of the psyche by the orientation of each particular culture, was a theme shared by Benedict and Mead, and led to the emergence of the subfield of **personality and culture**, which gave particular attention to enculturation and socialization of children.

NEO-BENEDICTINE THEORY

The most influential American anthropologist of the second half of the twentieth century, Clifford Geertz, began his research as a Parsonian. Talcott Parsons, in whose Department of Social Relations at Harvard Geertz did his graduate studies, was a major sociologist of mid-century. One of Parsons's (1937) main contributions was introducing to American academia Max Weber, the famous German sociologist. Parsons (1951, 1964) in his own work followed Weber, emphasizing the **voluntaristic** nature of goal-oriented human action. The Weberian theory as elaborated by Parsons analyzed the integrated human system of action into three analytic subsystems: the social system consisted of structures of roles and statuses that were functionally integrated; the personality system consisted of cognitions and emotions that were psychologically integrated; and the **cultural system** consisted of symbols characterized by logico-meaningful integration. Geertz (1973:ch. 6, originally published in 1959) was interested particularly in Parsons's cultural subsystem, which he saw as least understood in anthropology, but in the initial stages of his work continued to regard it as one of the three analytic subsystems in the Parsonian trinity.

Geertz (1973:ch. 4, originally published in 1966) makes a powerful case for focusing on symbols and the meanings conveyed through them in his early essay "Religion as a Cultural System." Here Geertz (1973:89) defines **culture** as

> an historically transmitted pattern of meanings embodied in symbols, a system of inherited conceptions expressed in symbolic forms by means of which men communicate, perpetuate, and develop their knowledge about and attitudes toward life.

This definition, which focuses on meanings and the symbols that convey them, is considerably narrower than the more global formulations of earlier anthropologists, such as Tylor's (1871) famous definition:

> Culture or Civilization, taken in its wide ethnographic sense, is that complex whole which includes knowledge, belief, art, morals, law, custom, and any other capabilities and habits acquired by man as a member of society.

Malinowski's ([1944] 1960) definition follows Tylor's, being "the integral whole consisting of implements and consumers" goods, of constitutional charters for the various social groupings, of human ideas and crafts, beliefs and customs." Benedict ([1935] 1961:33), while stressing integration of the parts, continues to use a global definition of culture: "A culture . . . is a more or less consistent pattern of thought and action." In contrast to these broader conceptions, Geertz leaves aside artifacts, behavior, personality, and institutions, focusing more narrowly on symbol systems and their meanings.

Geertz (1973:ch. 4) illustrates his approach with the example of religion, which he defines in terms of meaning and symbols:

> [A] religion is: (1) a system of symbols which acts to (2) establish powerful, pervasive, and long-lasting moods and motivations in men by (3) formulating conceptions of a general order of existence and (4) clothing these conceptions with such an aura of factuality that (5) the moods and motivations seem uniquely realistic. [original in italics]

Geertz elaborates on each of these five parts of his formulation. For example, discussing "conceptions of a general order of existence" he (1973:102–3) points out that people often have a

> persistent, constantly re-experienced difficulty in grasping certain aspects of nature, self, and society, in bringing certain elusive phenomena within the sphere of culturally formulatable fact, which renders [them] chronically uneasy

and religious formulations frame these elusive phenomena in understandable ways. So too the more concrete and intense challenge of suffering, pain, and death require placement in a broader context to be understandable and thus bearable. Geertz goes on to explore the complexities of religion as a system of meaning, drawing on a wide range of eclectic ethnographic and philosophical sources and making his case with the subtlety and the prose flourishes for which he is renowned.

Geertz's excursion into studying religion from the perspective of meaning and the symbols that carry it, rather than as behavior (e.g., praying, participating in rituals, avoiding forbidden acts), institutions (e.g., the church, shamans, ancestor worship), functional interrelatedness (e.g., ancestor worship upholds lineage organization, rituals channel emotions), or specific content (e.g., spirits, a supreme god, supernatural forces), offered a new model for anthropological research. Geertz (1973:ch. 8; 1983:ch. 4 and 5) used the template repeatedly: In "Ideology as a Cultural System," he (1973:220) argues that

> [w]hatever else ideologies may be—projections of unacknowledged fears, disguises for ulterior motives, phatic expressions of group solidarity—they are, most distinctively, maps of problematic social reality and matrices for the creation of collective conscience.

In "Common Sense as a Cultural System," he (1983:84) suggests that

> [c]ommon sense is not what the mind cleared of cant spontaneously apprehends; it is what the mind filled with presuppositions—that sex is a disorganizing force, that sex is a regenerative gift, that sex is a practical pleasure—concludes.

In "Art as a Cultural System," he (1983:119) proposes that

> [i]f there is a commonality [in art around the world] it lies in the fact that certain activities everywhere seem specifically designed to demonstrate that ideas are visible, audible, and . . . tactible, that they can be cast in forms where the senses, and through the senses the emotions, can reflectively address them. The variety of artistic expression stems from the variety of conceptions men have about the way things are, and is indeed the same variety.

Geertz thus instructs anthropology to focus on meanings and the various symbol systems that convey them.

In the course of his intellectual journey, Geertz (1973:ch. 1 passim; quote from p. 5) became convinced that culture is not one of three aspects of human action, but the very foundation of human life:

> The concept of culture I espouse . . . is essentially a semiotic one. Believing, with Max Weber, that man is an animal suspended in webs of significance he himself has spun, I take culture to be those webs, and the analysis of it to be therefore not an experimental science in search of law but an interpretive one in search of meaning. It is explication I am after, construing social expressions on their surface enigmatical.

In emphasizing explication, in contrast to explanation, Geertz (1973:14) distances himself from any idea of searching for the causes of culture or of attributing causes to culture. As did Benedict, Geertz (1963:ch. 1) sees culture as *sui generis*, a thing in itself, through which people understand and deal with the world; culture cannot be explained by, for example, environmental factors, because the parts of the environment with which people engage are defined, selected, and directed by their culture. Nor, for Geertz (1973:14), is culture itself a cause, for

> [a]s interworked systems of construable signs (. . . symbols), culture is not a power, something to which social events, behaviors, institutions,

or processes can be causally attributed; it is a context, something
within which they can be intelligibly—that is, thickly—described.

In fact, the main, really the only, task of anthropology, according to
Geertz (1973:ch. 1, passim), is description, particularly "thick description" (the phrase he uses for the title of his theoretical chapter). The
stock in trade of conventional anthropology—functional and causal
explanations, cross-cultural generalizations, theories about social differences and cultural evolution—are lain aside by Geertz (1973:ch. 1;
1983:ch. 3) in favor of ethnographic accounts of meaning "from the
native's point of view," effectively collapsing anthropology into ethnography. Furthermore, for Geertz ethnographic accounts are not privileged,
objective, scientific accounts, but interpretations, for "what we call our
data are really our own constructions of other people's constructions of
what they and their compatriots are up to" (Geertz 1973:9), and, as such,
are "fictions; fictions, in the sense that they are 'something made,' 'something fashioned'—the original meaning of *fictiō*" (Geertz 1973:15). Thick
description, then, is a result of interpretation, in fact interpretations of
interpretations. As a result, ethnographic accounts are "essentially con-
testable," open to debate. According to Geertz (1973:29),

> [a]nthropology, or at least interpretive anthropology, is a science
> whose progress is marked less by a perfection of consensus than by
> a refinement of debate. What gets better is the precision with which
> we vex each other.

What is accomplished by interpretive anthropology is "the enlargement
of the universe of human discourse" (Geertz 1973:14). It is not very sur-
prising that Geertz (1983) soon dropped the label of "science" and
began speaking more of the humanities, likening anthropological interpretation to literary criticism.

Geertz (1973:93, 216), not unlike Benedict, uses the phrase "culture patterns," although he seems to be referring to models or blue-
prints for aspects of particular cultures rather than for entire cultures.
He (1983:69) comes closer to Benedict when he describes the "herme-
neutic circle" of interpretation:

> In seeking to uncover the Javanese, Balinese, or Moroccan sense of
> self, one oscillates restlessly between the sort of exotic minutiae
> (lexical antitheses, categorical schemes, morpho-phonemic trans-
> formations) that make even the best ethnographies a trial to read
> and the sort of sweeping characterizations ("quietism," "drama-
> tism," "contextualism") that make all but the most pedestrian of
> them somewhat implausible.

These "sweeping characterizations" of Geertz's seem akin to Benedict's
conceptions of Apollonian ritualism in the Pueblos, Dionysian ecstasism
among the Plains Indians, malicious conflictualism on Dobu, and megalo-

maniac paranoia on the Northwest Coast. And although Geertz (1973:44) mentions Benedict only once in his first collection of essays, referring to *Patterns of Culture* as "probably the most popular book in anthropology ever published in this country," and not at all in his second collection, much of his later ethnographic work seems to have been inspired by the idea of a culture's central, ordering, dominant configuration.

THE SYMBOLICS OF POWER

Geertz's treatment of ethnographic cases as culture patterns or configurations is illustrated nicely in his comparison (1983:6) of the symbolics of authority in sixteenth-century England, fourteenth-century Java, and eighteenth- and nineteenth-century Morocco. He (1983:143, 146) approaches with the general argument, clearly an application of his general, heuristic model, that political power and authority and also rebellion always exist in a culturally specific context that provides the symbolic tools, the societal "master fictions," essential for self-definition and claims of legitimacy. The corollary is, of course, that in different cultures the symbolism of power differs.

One thing that Geertz finds present in all traditional kingdoms, or at least the three cases he describes, is "royal progresses" or extensive trips made to outlying parts of their realms by the king or queen accompanied by a large and elaborate royal retinue. These royal visits—in the absence of newspapers, radio, television, and the Internet—provide the occasion for the expression of symbolic claims by the king or queen on the loyalty or at least obedience of his or her subjects. The claims take the form of the contemporary "master fictions" or cultural themes upon which the social and political order are based. Let us see what Geertz has discovered about these three political cultures as they are expressed in "royal progresses."

During the inauguration of Elizabeth I of England and her subsequent royal progresses around the country, there are repeated performances, *tableau vivant*, and representations that show good triumphing over evil, religion over ignorance, justice over corruption, wisdom over folly. Elizabeth is called to be and presents herself as the royal personification of these virtues. The English

> imagination was allegorical, Protestant, didactic, and pictorial; it lived on moral abstractions cast into emblems. Elizabeth was Chastity, Wisdom, Peace, Perfect Beauty, and Pure Religion as well as queen . . . ; and being queen she was these things. (Geertz 1983:129)

Thus it was "pious and didactic" Christian moralism that provided the allegories for the "idealized passions" of English political culture (Geertz 1983:130, 134).

The Hayam Wuruk, king of Majapahit in eastern Java, Indonesia, represented the hierarchical pinnacle of human society and its connection with the gods above. The spatial arrangements of the royal court, the capital city, the kingdom, and (in the minds of those who shared this "fiction") all other countries of the world reflected this cosmic hierarchy (Geertz 1983:ch. 6; 1980).

> The basic principle of Indonesian statecraft [was] that the court should be a copy of the cosmos and the realm a copy of the court, with the king, liminally suspended between gods and men, the mediating image in both directions. (1983:130)

During royal progresses, the elaborate procession of thousands, with hundreds of ox carts, horses, donkeys, camels, and elephants, was organized spatially so that all parties were in their proper places, the four ranking princesses arranged according to the quarter of the kingdom they represented, and the king in the center, shining in gold and jewels. The magnificence and the hierarchy reflecting, according to local culture, the cosmos. Thus it was Indic aestheticism that provided the analogical basis for the "hierarchical and mystical" Javanese political culture as a "continuum of spiritualized pride" (Geertz 1983:130, 134).

In Morocco, the king had to impose himself actively on a society in which the guiding principle was that

> one genuinely possesses only what one has the ability to defend, whether it be land, water, women, trade partners, or personal authority: whatever magic a king had he had strenuously to protect. (1983:136)

Power was seen as a personal characteristic that reflected God's favor, and the ability to force others to do one's bidding a proof of power and at the same time a justification of power. The king of Morocco, like many of his subjects, was nomadic, shifting between four royal cities and otherwise traveling from region to region, place to place in the countryside, meeting, hosting, feasting, bribing, punishing, colluding, threatening, rewarding, and sometimes fighting but always asserting his suzerainty over the local population and local leaders.

> The mobility of the king was thus a central element in his power; the realm was unified—to the very partial degree that it was unified and was a realm—by a restless searching-out of contact, mostly agonistic, with literally hundreds of lesser centers of power within it. (Geertz 1983:138)

The political culture of "agonistic" Morocco was thus based upon "explosions of divine energy" (Geertz 1983:142).

As Geertz (1983:138) sums it up, "What chastity was to Elizabeth, and magnificence to Hayam Wuruk, energy was to Mulay Ismail or Mulay Hasan. . . ." In England political culture expressed "embodiments of redemptive virtue," in Java "reflections of cosmic order," and in Morocco "explosions of divine energy" (Geertz 1983:142). In a nutshell, English society was moralistic, Javanese aesthetic, and Moroccan agonistic. These patterns, as characterized by Geertz, are the basic configurations, the spirits, the essences of these societies. For there is no valid distinction between "trappings" and "substance," for "they are transformed into each other" (Geertz 1983:124).

Geertz, in the course of seeking essences (see also Geertz 1968, 1979, 1988), makes many sensitive ethnographic excursions and provides his readers with highly suggestive vignettes and astute observations. If his cultural analysis is incisive, his writing is rich, complex, sometimes convoluted, and a Henry Jamesian performance in its own right, with frequent (and much appreciated) offerings of the witty turn of phrase and *bon mot*. His (1988) interest in "the anthropologist as author" is very much in character. Geertz is thus not only a student of symbol systems, he himself is also a master of symbols.

DEEP STRUCTURE

The Maasai (Spear and Waller 1993) of Kenya in East Africa are a tall, proud, striking people. Today as in the past, many Maasai reside in villages on their own territory and make a living by raising cattle that graze the grasslands of the open range. The Maasai nourish themselves by drinking the milk of their cattle and only rarely, on ceremonial occasions, eat meat. Maasai men organize themselves by age, divided into (a) uninitiated boys, (b) unmarried, spear-carrying warriors who reside with the cattle in pasture, (c) married elders who manage household production and direct community politics, and (d) retired men.

For most Maasai, there is only one proper way to live, as a pastoralist, raising cattle, which are central not only to Maasai practical life but also to Maasai symbolic, aesthetic, ritual life. And yet there are among the Maasai several groups who follow other occupations: the Il-Torrobo hunters, the Il-Kunono blacksmiths, and the Il-Oibonok diviners (Galaty 1979). These groups are not only regarded as separate from the ordinary Maasai pastoralists and seen as somehow problematical, but the hunters and blacksmiths are strongly disparaged and deemed by the pastoralists inferior. How can we understand these social divisions and differential evaluations? John G. Galaty (1979) draws on **structuralist** analysis to elicit the symbolic basis of the inequality among Maasai.

Galaty (1979) argues that below the surface relations of these groups there are underlying conceptions and values which inform and direct their mutual understandings and disagreements. These conceptions are called the structure of Maasai culture. (However, to distinguish this culture or conceptual structure from the more behavioral and organizational "social structure" of the British structural functionalists, I will refer to it as **deep structure**. This phraseology is consistent with some structuralists' views that culture structure is a reflection of the structure of the brain and even the structure of the universe.) Many of these conceptions refer to cattle, because cattle are so central to Maasai life (Galaty 1979:808–9). In other words, cattle are a major symbol that plays an important part in Maasai conceptions of themselves and the world. (In case you are wondering, there is no known historical connection between the culture of sacred cattle in India and Maasai culture.) How do ideas about cattle set the stage for social relations of differentiation and disparagement?

Maasai pastoralists see themselves as defenders of cattle and producers and consumers of milk and butter. In contrast, hunters do not protect animals for a living, but kill for a living, and live on meat. While the hands of pastoralists are clean, the hands of hunters are bloody.

	PASTORALISM	HUNTING
animal life:	protecting	killing
consumption:	milk	meat
purity:	clean	bloody

Blacksmiths engage in dirty and degrading work and produce dangerous iron implements such as knives, spears, and razors.

	PASTORALISM	BLACKSMITHING
labor:	dignified	degrading
person:	clean	dirty
blood:	conserving	shedding

Diviners are in touch with the supernatural, and have the ability to see the unknown, to influence the future, and to offer ritual protection. They provide powerful ritual medicines made from roots, bark, and leaves. Diviners facilitate dangerous, generative events and constructive bloodletting, such as birth, initiation, and sacrifice.

	PASTORALISM	DIVINING
consumption:	milk	mead (honey beer)
powers:	human	supernatural
position:	earthbound	liminal
effects:	conserving	generative

Galaty (1979:809–10) sums up the Maasai world as seen from the point of view of the pastoralists:

> . . .[D]iviners and pastoralists represent . . . the forces of a well-in-
> tentioned culture, maintaining a God-given pattern of dignified
> and restrained activity against the forces of a malicious nature and
> the bestiality of [meat-eating] gluttony and [bloodletting] destruc-
> tion. Pollution [the negative evaluation of the pastoralists about
> the hunters and blacksmiths] is here associated with the harbin-
> gers of destruction, the hunters and blacksmiths, who are depreci-
> ated as bloodshed is to peace, evil to Godliness, disorder to order,
> and selfishness to sociability. An unrestrained nature is kept at bay
> by a dignified culture, the shedding of blood abjured for the aim of
> its preservation.

The pastoralists thus look down on the hunters and the blacksmiths, even while they might benefit from the activities of these despised groups, and look up with awe to the diviners, albeit with some fear as well. The result is that the Maasai pastoralists tend to keep their distance from these other Maasai groups. For example, the blacksmiths are said to have "bitter blood," and other Maasai avoid sexual and marital contact with them for fear of contagion and contamination.

Even from this oversimplified summary of parts of Galaty's (1979) complex and subtle account of the Maasai, it is clear that the relations between the pastoralists and the hunters, blacksmith, and diviners are not accidental, or fortuitous, or the result of simple facts of realpolitik or wealth. Whatever the origin of the split between the pastoralists and these other groups, contemporary relations are underpinned and reinforced by a set of structured, symbolic conceptions that describe and evaluate the basic elements in life. Furthermore, these conceptions appear to be structured in paired oppositions or binary concepts such as human/supernatural, clean/dirty, life/death, and so forth. Eliciting this deep symbolic structure allows us to explicate the social patterns found in daily life.

This structural analysis derives from the seminal work of Claude Lévi-Strauss, the standard bearer from French philosophy, and the most influential continental anthropologist during the second half of the twentieth century. As we will recall, for the British structural functionalists, social structure consisted of the actual social relations in a society, or the ongoing social relations, or the relationships between groups in a society. In contrast, for Lévi-Strauss, the structure is the basic organizing principle that underlies the order in a particular society. This principle, the deep structure, is conceptual, taking the form of paired oppositions, or **binary concepts**, such as nature/culture, male/female, inside/outside, and life/death. This conceptual cultural order parallels that of language, particularly phonemics, which is based on contrasts resulting from paired oppositions of sound, such as p/b, k/q, d/t, p/t, p/k, and k/t. Lévi-Strauss (1963:ch. 2, 4) drew on the basic model of structural linguistics and developed it for the study of cultures, applying it especially to kinship ([1949] 1969, 1963:ch. 2, 4, 7, 8), myth (1963:ch.11, [1964] 1969, 1966, 1968), and classification ([1962] 1966). According to Lévi-Strauss, binary concepts underlie language and culture because this is the way the human brain is structured, and, as the brain evolved as part of the wider universe, the brain must itself reflect the structure of the universe.

A tired cliché in the history of Western philosophy is the opposition between British empiricism and French **rationalism**. But it is tired because it has had to do so much work over the years, and it will not be given any rest here, because we too must apply it to the development of theory about cohesion in culture. Lévi-Strauss is a rationalist in at least four senses: One is that, unlike empiricists, who seek knowledge by direct observation of the world, relying on "sense data" to provide the basic information needed, Lévi-Strauss seeks truth deep under the empirical surface and relies on his own mind to identify and analyze basic patterns. The second way that Lévi-Strauss is a rationalist is that he focuses on cognition, thought, as the basis of society and culture, downplaying emotion, sentiment, and the nonrational drives (Spiro 1979). The third way is that (at the very least he speaks most of the time as if) he does not believe that how people live determines how they think, but rather believes that how people think determines how they live. The fourth is that Lévi-Strauss is not primarily interested in how particular societies work, or the similarities and differences among cultures, but is mainly interested in how examining various cultures can inform us about the commonalities of the human psyche, about the human mind that we all share. As Leach (1970:51, emphasis in original) puts it, Lévi-Strauss's quest "is to discover the collective *unconscious* of 'the human mind' (*l'espirit humain*)." This focus on the unconscious distinguishes Lévi-Strauss from his famous French predecessor, Emile Durkheim ([1893] 1933:79)—to whom Lévi-Strauss dedicated his collection *Structural Anthropology*—a founder of sociology and anthropology, who discussed the "collective consciousness" (*conscience collective*), the beliefs and sentiments common among members of a society, which many readers would gloss as "culture."

Let us see how Lévi-Strauss applies his structuralist approach to a famous cultural (or, more accurately, anthropological) phenomenon: totemism. The word "totem" is derived from the Ojibwa, an Algonkian language of North America (Lévi-Strauss [1962] 1969:86). The Ojibwa word is *ototeman*, which means "he is a relative of mine" and expressed clan membership. A clan is an exclusive kinship group in which the members are descended from a common human or nonhuman ancestor. Clans are also exogamous, which means that one must marry out. In many places around the world where clans are found, the clans are represented and identified by animals or other natural phenomena that are thought to be their apical and common ancestors. For example, the five great Ojibwa clans were the catfish, crane, loon, bear, and marten (Lévi-Strauss [1962] 1969:87).

Anthropologists in the nineteenth and early twentieth centuries, such as Sir James Frazier, Goldenweiser, and van Gennep, had been fascinated with this identification of people with animals and had seen, or thought they had seen, a totemism institutional complex (Lévi-Strauss [1962] 1969:introduction). These anthropologists described totemism as having several essential characteristics (often three were mentioned)—such as clans with exclusive membership, exogamy, totems associated with clans, taboos on harming the totems, and so forth—but often disagreed on exactly which elements made up the basic totemism complex. Subsequent research showed that each element of the so-called totemism complex was widespread and was combined in various places with none, one, two, or all other elements of the "complex" and many other elements as well. So from the mid-twentieth century most anthropologists recognized that there was not a single totemism institutional complex, but rather that the use of animal symbols in social organization was widespread and diverse.

The nineteenth-century anthropologists who had identified what they thought was a totemism complex saw it within an evolutionary framework as characteristic of an earlier period of human evolution when people's ideas and understandings were simple. This approach was effectively refuted by Goldenweiser in 1910 (Leach 1970:41). Thereafter, until Lévi-Strauss, anthropologists focused on the uses of the animals identified as totems and the benefits for the society of controlling their use. One functionalist explanation for the identification with animal totems was that the taboo on eating one's animal ancestor had the function of providing protection and thus conservation for that species, an approach somewhat sarcastically characterized by critics as being the "totemic animals were good to eat" theory.

Lévi-Strauss's ([1962] 1969; [1962] 1966:ch. 2–4) structuralist approach brings to totemism a different framework and different presumptions. At the most general level, a set of animal totems and categories is seen as one part of a much broader and more complex classification system that is a basic part of every culture. According to Lévi-Strauss (1966:9–10), human beings all share an "intellectual requirement" of finding order in the world. In looking at people's assertions about the different elements of the world and their connections, the first question is not whether their assertion is the most efficacious, but rather

> whether some initial order can be introduced into the universe by means of these groupings. Classifying, as opposed to not classifying, has a value of its own, whatever form the classification may take. . . . The thought we call primitive is founded on this demand for order. This is equally true of all thought but it is through the

properties common to all thought that we can most easily begin to understand forms of thought which seem very strange to us.

The "totemic" linkage between human groups and animals—"we are the catfish; they are the loons"—may seem very strange to us (unless of course we are fans of the Chicago Bears, the Baltimore Orioles, or the Anaheim Mighty Ducks), but we can understand the linkage better, according to structuralism, if we focus on the structure rather than the content.

After all, it is not that Chicago football players are substantively (anatomically, behaviorally, visually) like bears, while Baltimore Ravens players are birdlike. As Lévi-Strauss (1966:148) says,

> . . . [I]n none of these cases can the animal, the "totem" or its species be grasped as a biological entity: . . . [rather] the animal appears [i.e., is used as] as a conceptual tool . . .

Chicago and Baltimore football players, really very much alike (and some, from one time to another, shifting from one team to the other), are distinguished from one another for the purposes of team play, just as bears and ravens can be distinguished from one another. In other words, it is not the connection between the Chicago team and the bear that is critical for the working of football, but the two parallel systems of differences:

Bear————Raven————Panther———Lion ————Ram
Chicago——Baltimore——Carolina——Detroit——St. Louis

The classification system of distinct animal totems parallels the series of similar football teams and both distinguishes the teams one from another and binds them into the unity of a broader, inclusive system made up of substantively similar but symbolically unique units in a unified football league. Football is my example, but the analysis is that of Lévi-Strauss ([1962] 1966) as he explains "so-called totemic institutions":

> The homology [that totemic institutions] evoke is not between social groups and natural species but between the differences which manifest themselves on the level of groups on the one hand and on that of species on the other. They are thus based on the postulate of a homology between *two systems of differences*, one of which occurs in nature and the other in culture. (p. 115; emphasis in original)
> . . .*[I]t is not the resemblances* [between groups of people and animals], *but the differences which resemble each other.* (Lévi-Strauss [1962] 1969:149, emphasis in original)

A series of animal differences is conceived as paralleling a series of social groups because this aids cognitively in the distinction and the relating of the social groups. In reality, these groups are human groups and, through a rule of exogamous marriage, exchange sisters and daughters with one another. The identification of groups with animal species symbolically gives the illusion that each group is a different species from the other and is supplying women of its particular species. These social groups thus draw symbolically on the real differences of the natural order for establishing relations of complementarity and cooperation among themselves. In other words, men conceive these relations on the model of their conception of the relations between natural species (and at the same time their own social relations). People use their model of differences between natural species to order their social world and rationalize their organization of intergroup relations. But the use of animal species to represent social groups does more: it unifies the divergent worlds of culture and nature, and unifies them into one total system. It is for these reasons that Lévi-Strauss ([1962] 1969:132, 162) famously said that natural species are chosen as totems not because they are good to eat, but because they are good to think.

In considering different kinds of societies and cultures, structuralists go beyond juxtaposing the different symbolic structures and noting their distinctiveness and diversity. As well, they examine the way in which one culture structure can be seen as a **transformation** of another, quite different one. For example, let us consider what happens when identification with natural species is taken literally, and, instead of the differences between species serving as a model for differences between clans, as in totemism, each social group identifies itself (whether or not through reference to an animal or other totem) as a natural species and thus incapable due to the laws of nature of reproducing with one another? The result is endogamy, marrying only within the group (which is the opposite of exogamy). Each group sees itself as a nature species, a different world and different nature from each other group. Where can we find such groups? The classic example is the **castes** of South Asia, each of which has its own organization, rules, customs, practices, rituals, and beliefs, and each of which allows marriage only within the group. As there is no exchange of people between castes, how do people of different castes relate with one another, and how is the society as a whole organized and integrated? Different castes are assigned different cultural tasks—priest, soldier, farmer, herder, trader, blacksmith, leather worker, cleaner—and each caste performs its special role for all of the others and the society as a whole. The social complementarity between castes exists in reality, in the different jobs performed, and so interdependence is guaranteed without marriage exchange. As Lévi-Strauss ([1962] 1966:125) puts it,

> Castes are heterogeneous in function [jobs] and can therefore be homogeneous [and separate] in structure: since the diversity of function is real, complementarity is already established on the level of reality and the operation of marriage exchanges ... would be ... of no practical value. ... Conversely, totemic groups are homogeneous

so far as their function [jobs] is concerned, for it [the exchange of women] makes no real yield and amounts to no more than a repetition of the same illusion for all the groups. They therefore have to be [conceived of as] heterogeneous in structure, each being destined for the production of women of a different social species.

Totemic groups and castes are not exactly opposites, because symbolically construed differences are not the same as actual practiced differences. But totemic groups and castes can be seen as transformations of the same underlying structure. As Lévi-Strauss ([1962] 1966:127) puts it,

> [W]e can on a very general plane perceive an equivalence between the two main systems of differences to which men have had recourse for conceptualizing their social relations. Simplifying a great deal, it may be said that castes picture themselves as a natural species while totemic groups picture natural species as castes. And this must be refined: castes naturalize a true culture falsely, totemic groups culturalize a false nature truly.

That is, castes are truly different from one another in culture, but they falsely pretend that these real differences make them like different natural species. In contrast, totemic groups pretend that marriage exchanges can take place between different species, but they really do engage in actual marriage exchange. A lot seems to arise, as Lévi-Strauss argues, from the way people conceptualize the relations between nature and culture.

The structuralist approach is also highly suitable for application to texts, and Lévi-Strauss (1963, [1964] 1969, 1966, 1968) has energetically and masterfully applied it to myths and rituals from cultures around the world. Among the literally hundreds of myths and rituals examined, each explored with extensive commentary and multiple cross-references for its underlying structural "mythologic," is an examination of rituals related to marriage order. For illustration, I want to point out only one main argument made by Lévi-Strauss ([1964] 1969:334–37) as part of his much more complicated and subtle analysis.

In rural France, it was expected that the elder children in the family marry before the younger. When, as it sometimes happened, younger children married before elder, while the elder was still single, this cultural rule was violated and there was a sense of anomaly. In many districts there were customs that addressed this anomaly. Lévi-Strauss ([1964] 1969:334) quotes an account by Van Gennep:

> If a younger daughter was married first, this was a sad day for her poor elder sister, for at some point during the celebrations, she would, willy-nilly, be seized upon, lifted up and laid on the top of the oven, so that she might be warmed up, as the saying was, since her situation seemed to indicate that she had remained insensitive to love.

Elsewhere in France and also in England, the response to the same anomaly was treated differently. In England the unmarried elder sister had to dance barefoot, while elsewhere in France, the unmarried elder brother and sister had to eat a salad of onions, roots, clover, and/or oats.

Lévi-Strauss ([1964]1969:335) argues that the custom of putting an unmarried elder sibling on an oven was not about warming them up sexually. Rather, if we look at the customs together, we can see that the unmarried elder siblings are either forced to confront "the raw," as in dancing barefoot or eating uncooked salad, or to be exposed to heat from an oven, and thus "cooked." Such exposure is widespread elsewhere, as in Asia where after giving birth a new mother was placed on a grill or bed under which a slow fire burned, or in Pueblo Indian communities among which women gave birth over a heap of hot sand, just as Californian tribes put women who had given birth into ovens hollowed out in the ground and covered with mats and hot stones. Why is this done? According to Lévi-Strauss ([1964] 1969:336, emphasis in original)

> the individuals who are "cooked" are those deeply involved in a physiological process: the newborn child, the woman who has just given birth, . . . The conjunction of a member of the social group with nature must be mediatized [mediated] through the intervention of cooking fire, whose normal function is to mediatize the conjunction of the raw product and the human consumer, and whose operation thus has the effect of making sure that a natural creature is at one and the same time *cooked and socialized*. . . .

The "raw" thus stands for nature, while the "cooked" stands for culture:

$$raw : cooked :: nature : culture$$

Returning now to our unmarried elder siblings, we can see, thanks to structural analysis, that in the rather rude wedding customs reported above, these individuals and their communities are reminded of their deviant, anticultural behavior either by being forced to eat raw food or by displaying themselves publicly "in the raw" by dancing barefoot, or they are forcibly put on a stove so that they can be cooked and thus socialized into proper cultural behavior. Deviant behavior is thus symbolically likened to savage, untamed nature, while behavior conforming to the norms is lauded as civilized, cultural behavior. From this structural analysis we can see these customs—at first appearance cruel and senseless—as serious social commentaries on deviant behavior.

Lévi-Strauss shares with Geertz and Benedict a focus on explication of meaning. Cultural analysis—whether structuralist, interpretationalist, or configurationalist—aims at eliciting the meaning contained in symbols and thus contextualizing human actions within the frameworks of significance—about the nature of the world and about what is desirable and undesirable—that people require for guidance about how to think and feel and act. Through examining this cultural contextualization, people's lives and actions can be understood and appreciated. No causal explanation is intended or expected from cultural analysis. Rather, people are to be understood in their humanity as meaning-bearing and creating, with culture as both context and collective achievement.

Chapter Six

Transformation through Time
History and Evolution

The birth of anthropology, its origin, its foundation, is in evolution. Anthropology, it can justly be said, is a child of evolution. It was evolution, in three senses of the term, that inspired the birth of anthropology in the nineteenth century: the technological revolution in Europe; the Enlightenment; and the idea of Progress.

THE TECHNOLOGICAL REVOLUTION IN EUROPE

One evolution was the transformation of western European economy and society during the eighteenth and first half of the nineteenth centuries, from around 1700 to 1850. The age-old agrarian society in Europe, based upon a rural population engaged largely in subsistence agriculture, was radically transformed during this 150-year period into an industrializing society with a large urban population and a strong industrial sector, supported by a developed transportation and communication infrastructure. This was a result of multiple and ingenious innovations and improvements in agricultural, manufacturing, and infrastructural technology.

Agriculture, after centuries if not millennia of stagnancy, was transformed by practices that led to a much higher level of productivity (Williams 1964:203–8). The broadcasting of seed to plant crops was replaced by row cultivation, allowing tending of plants during growth, when Jethro Tull (died 1742) invented the seed drill. Special fodder crops for animals, the use of manure for fertilization of all agricultural crops, and field rotation of wheat, turnips, barley, and clover, eliminating fallow periods, were developed by Charles, Viscount Townshend (died 1738). Profits from agriculture increased as much as 400 percent in the period following these innovations. These new profits from agriculture provided capital investment for industry and fueled the development of manufacturing.

The evolution of livestock production was equally impressive. Before 1700, sheep and cattle were small and raised for wool and dairy products; meat was rare. Intensive selective breeding led to the doubling of size during the eighteenth century. At Smithfield, oxen sold in 1710 averaged 370 lbs., while those sold in 1795 averaged 800 lbs.; sheep sold in 1710 averaged 38 lbs., while those sold in 1795 averaged 80 lbs.

Mass communication contributed to agricultural development. Information about new agricultural methods was diffused widely by print, such as the *Annals of Agriculture*, established in 1784. In 1793, King George III of England set up a Board of Agriculture to publicize new agricultural and land management techniques.

The shift from traditional open field, strip-farming to block enclosures led to larger scale farming, increased productivity, and greater profits. Small holders were pushed out of agriculture and many abandoned the countryside. In 1700, 80 percent of the English lived in the countryside, with only 20 percent in towns; by 1760, 30 percent of the English had shifted from the countryside to the towns, so that of the total population, 50 percent remained in the countryside while 50 percent lived in towns, thus providing a new labor force for industry. During this same period, the death rate declined due to better sanitation (e.g., use of soap), better nutrition (e.g., consumption of meat and vegetables), better architecture (e.g., slate for thatch), and more effective medicine and midwifery, and this led to an increasing population.

Advances in industry (Williams 1964:210–15) were even more breathtaking. The first true factory was established by Thomas Lombe in 1717 to house machines driven by water power for throwing silk. In 1733, John Kay invented the flying shuttle for weaving wool. The first steam engine was built by Thomas Newcomen to pump water from coal mines. Thomas Watt built a much improved version in 1765, which was used also to drive the wheels in the developing iron industry. The production of coal, used for fueling industrial machines, increased fourfold, from 2.5 million tons to 10 million tons, during the years between 1700 to 1800. The textile industry expanded with the spinning jenny in 1760, the spinning frame in 1768, the power-driven carding machine in 1775, the multipurpose spinner in the 1780s, and new techniques for bleaching and dyeing, which made possible production of cheap cottons for the general public (and led to the general use of underwear for the first time).

The muddy paths for packhorses that had provided transportation for millennia were replaced by new forms of transport necessary for moving materials for the new industries. Canals were widely built between 1760 and 1830 (an exercise that was the origin of the profession of civil engineering) and used for hauling heavy industrial materials. After 1850, packhorses were replaced by wagons as a result of road building. John McAdam (1756–1836) made the first hard surface, "macadam" roads. Railroads, at first on wooden rails and drawn by horses, were built in the mid-1700s to carry coal and iron from mines to canals. By 1767, iron rails were used, and in the 1800s, steam power.

In sum, the English and other western Europeans following them saw their economies and societies (even leaving aside the momentous political changes) transformed radically in the eighteenth and nineteenth centuries. From age-old agrarian societies run in conventional ways, they had become consciously innovative, technologically advanced, highly productive, urbanized, industrialized, mass producing, evolved societies. This remarkable development, as one can imagine, did not go unnoticed but became a central element in Western reflection on the nature of society and culture, and humanity.

THE SCIENTIFIC REVOLUTION

The second evolution that underlay the birth of anthropology was the transformation of knowledge that we call (with no bias, of course) the Enlightenment. The Enlightenment was a major shift in worldview, or *weltanschauung*, in the underlying **paradigm** of what counts as knowledge and of how to gain that knowledge. Ever since the earliest civilizations, as long as ten thousand years ago, agrarian civilizations had developed (different versions of) a sacred worldview, based on the idea that human life, the world, and the universe were determined by the actions of powerful, superhuman, supernatural beings, by gods or God, and lesser supernatural agents. This worldview assumed a static, permanent, perfect world created by supernatural forces, a world unchanging except for direct interventions by gods, God, or agents of God. For example, the ancient Greek philosopher Aristotle (384–322 B.C.), said that ". . . the sun and the stars are born not, neither do they decay, but are eternal and divine" (quoted in Greene 1996:14). The world and other species existed, in this vision, for human beings and their struggles to meet God's or the gods' demands. Humans were believed to be the central features of earth, the earth the center of the solar system, and the solar system the center of the universe. Knowledge and truth were to be found in one source and one source alone, the sacred texts.

The (European) Enlightenment was the breaking away from the sacred, religious paradigm, its method of gaining knowledge through the authoritative holy texts, and its supernaturally based view of existence. In place of the sacred paradigm was one based upon direct observation, on examination through the human senses of the world, the animal kingdom, mankind, and the universe, and then the formation of understandings, explanations, and theories based on those observations. As Robert Hooke (quoted in Greene 1996:48) said in 1694,

> . . . 'tis a vain thing to make experiments and collect Observations, if when we have them, we may not make use of them; . . . I hope that sensible Evidence and Reason may at length prevail against Prejudice, . . .

Observation and evidence became the new standards of knowledge. New techniques for observation were born with the invention of the telescope and the microscope, and the use of excavation for uncovering land formations and fossils, and the juxtaposing of individuals and of species in comparative anatomy. People began seeing things that no one had ever seen before. The new techniques led to the observations—all contrary to religiously based, traditional assertions—that the earth was not at the center of the solar system; that the earth had not remained stable but had changed radically and was continuing to change; that plant and animal species were not created for all time, but arose at different times and died out at different times; and that the lengthy history of the earth and the relatively short history of mankind did not coincide.

The new Enlightenment paradigm came to conclusions radically different from the previous sacred paradigm: First, the world could be best understood as systems of matter in motion following the laws of nature. Second, the earth had changed over time as a result of ongoing processes at work today, an assumption called the **uniformitarian** thesis, in contrast to the **catastrophist** thesis that the earth changed as God intervened and sent floods or other forces. Third, the natural world was not created for conscious purposes but evolved as a result of changes in matter in response to changing conditions. Fourth, mankind is not a creation distinct and separate from the rest of nature, but rather a recent development—very similar to other primates—of the same forces that produced the rest of existence. Fifth and finally, morality has no meaning in nature, which operates according to its own laws, but only in human society. These five tenets of the Enlightenment paradigm make up, to use another label, the scientific model of the world that (together with the associated scientific method) has provided the knowledge for subsequent technological developments—such as industrial mass production, electricity, aeronautics, pharmaceuticals, and electronic mass communications—in modern society.

The Enlightenment also brought a major change in social thought (Williams 1964:79–91). While the old, Christian sacred worldview directed people to focus on other-worldly salvation, the new, Enlightenment focus was this-worldly, emphasizing human life on earth. "Knowledge was directed toward endowing human life with greater comfort and power . . ." (Williams 1964:83). This was conceptualized in the seminal idea of "progress":

> Here we arrive at a fundamental characteristic of eighteenth-century intellectuals: whether rationalists or empiricists, whether optimistic or seemingly pessimistic, they were concerned for the progress of man on this earth and regarded such progress as possible. (Williams 1964:86)

What was the fruit of this intellectual seed?

THE THEORY OF EVOLUTION

Enlightenment thought about nature and the earth had crystalized by the early nineteenth century into theories of evolution. The temporal development of geological forms, resulting from uniform natural forces operating over long periods of time—the "uniformitarian" approach—was set out in Charles Lyell's *Principles of Geology, Being an Attempt to Explain the Former Changes of the Earth's Surface by Reference to Causes Now in Operation* (four volumes, 1830–1833) (Eisley 1959:ch. 4; Greene 1996:ch. 9). This was followed in 1859 by Charles Darwin's evolutionary theory, set out in *The Origin of Species*, which argued that changes in species over time resulted from natural selection in the competitive struggle for existence. The specific case of the evolution of the human species was taken up in 1863 by Lyell in *The Geological Evidences of the Antiquity of Man with Remarks on Theories of the Origin of Species by Variation*, and in 1874 by Darwin in *The Descent of Man, and Selection in Relation to Sex.*

It stood to reason that if the earth, plants, animals, and the human species evolved over time, so too did society and culture. Theories of the evolution of society and culture were formulated in response to a set of apparently undeniable facts. One such fact was that societies, cultures, and peoples change over time, as clearly demonstrated by the evolution of Western European society from the dark ages through the Renaissance, the Reformation, the Industrial Revolution, to advanced, nineteenth-century civilization. The second was that Western European society had grown and was growing, in overall population, population density, settlement size, transportation networks, agricultural and industrial production, and consequent wealth. The third was that Western European society had become more complex, in scientific knowledge; in agricultural, industrial, and medical practice; in occupational division of labor; and in social class differentiation. The fourth was that European society had not just grown larger and more complex, but it had improved in quality, demonstrating **progress**, in increased health and longevity, knowledge and education, standard of living (underwear!), enlightened religion, and enlightened, representative government. Furthermore, and this is the fifth and "confirming" fact, European explorers, adventurers, merchants, and missionaries had for over two hundred years diffused throughout the world and found a great variety of divergent societies and cultures, ranging from handfuls of individuals with rudimentary if any dwellings and stone tools, up to large, densely populated, agrarian civilizations with complex social hierarchies and elaborate literary traditions. It was obvious, or appeared to the evolutionists to be, that these variant societies could be placed in a developmental sequence, along with the different developmental phases of European society, which would illustrate the ascent of society and culture.

The contact between Europeans and non-European societies, and anthropology's subsequent focus on non-European societies, has led some late-twentieth-century commentators (e.g., Asad 1973; Hymes 1969) to assert, not without some political motivation, that anthropology was a child of imperialism. While it is true that the expansion of European influence provided ease of opportunity for anthropological research among non-European peoples, evolution was the formative influence on anthropology and its twin, sociology, and was the most powerful factor in its emergence.

THE EVOLUTION OF CULTURE

Herbert Spencer, in 1860 (1996:16), argued that we could understand the evolution of society by seeing its parallels to biological organisms, which were "[t]hat societies slowly augment in mass; that they progress in complexity of structure; that at the same time their parts become more mutually dependent. . . ." The evolution of European society and the history of human culture overall seemed to illustrate these processes.

Edward Burnett Tylor, in *Primitive Culture*, published in 1871 (1996:26–40), famously provided the first anthropological definition of culture:

> Culture or Civilization, taken in its wide ethnographic sense, is that complex whole which includes knowledge, belief, art, morals, law, custom, and any other capabilities and habits acquired by man as a member of society.

Tylor ([1871] 1996:27) argued that we can understand human society only by recognizing

> the unity of nature, the fixity of its laws, the definite sequence of cause and effect through which every fact depends on what has gone before it, and acts upon what is to come after it.

This, he continued, would allow us to explain the uniformities so widespread throughout cultures, and also the differences among cultures as "stages of development or evolution each the outcome of previous history" (p. 27). The methods were, first, to look for customs that were "survivals" from earlier stages of development, in order to tell us about a culture's past, and, second, the examination of contemporary societies, such as hunting, pastoral, and horticultural peoples, whose way of life corresponds to a substantial degree with our ancient ancestors. The result of this inquiry would be to reconstruct the evolution of human culture "from savagery to civilization" (Tylor [1871] 1996:37). Although for Tylor there were no racial differences in capability, for mankind shared a common origin and unity, he believed societies developed from the simple to the complex, and religious practice evolved toward greater rationality, although rationality was for him clearly discernable in even "simple" religions such as **animism**.

Lewis Henry Morgan, writing in *Ancient Society*, published in 1877 (1996:41–51), also took the view that the human brain was the same everywhere and that therefore societies and cultures would develop in much the same ways according to the conditions in which they existed. Morgan drew a developmental scheme that would categorize societies by their technologies. Lower, middle, and upper savagery were defined respectively by the use of fish, fire, and the bow and arrow. Lower, middle, and upper barbarism were defined by the use of pottery, irrigation cultivation and animal domestication, and iron. And the highest category, civilization, was defined by the use of writing. Each category might be characterized by certain other features such as, in middle barbarism, housing made with adobe-brick and stone construction. The categories of the development scheme are considered sequential, but they are not temporal or historical periods, for different societies are found in these different "conditions," or levels of technological development, at the same time, during the same historical period.

Marx and Engels set out their evolutionary framework in *The German Ideology*, published in 1845–1846 (1996:52–65). They focused on changes in the **social relations of production**, which involved examination of who owns what, who does what work, and who gets what at the end. Production was deemed central because human beings, as members of a natural species living in the natural world, had to attend to their biological needs for food, clothing, and shelter as an absolute necessity, so producing those necessities would therefore be the foundation of human cultural life. It is for this reason that they state that "[l]ife is not determined by consciousness, but consciousness by life" (p. 58); that is, people's ideas do not determine the material conditions in which people live, rather it is the material conditions in which people live that produce their ideas. As we have seen in chapter 4, many twentieth-century anthropologists have been influenced by the materialist theory of Marx and Engels.

Marx and Engels's evolutionary argument was that social relations of production are related to the **forces of production**, such as the natural resources and the technology used, and that developing forces of production can lead to contradictions with the social relations of production, and that this can lead to class conflict and changes in the established social relations. Their evolutionary scheme set out five basic stages of development: The first was based upon tribal ownership of the means of production and characterized by tribal organization and patriarchal chieftains. The second is ancient communal and state ownership, characterized by supra-tribal organization and a laboring class of slaves. The third is feudal ownership based on a hierarchy of nobles, armed retainers, and enserfed peasant producers. The fourth is capitalist ownership of the means of production, with owners at the top and propertyless workers selling their labor. The (projected, but not extant) fifth and final is communist collective ownership characterized by a classless society.

Throughout the late nineteenth and early twentieth centuries, the evolution of culture and society remained as primary preoccupation of social theorists. Ferdinand Tönnies ([1887] 1957:part 1) conceptualized the transformation as from *gemeinschaft*, community, thought of as intimate, organic sociality, characteristic of rural life, to *gesellschaft*, society, thought of as an impersonal, mechanical structure, characteristic of urban life.

> All intimate, private, and exclusive living together . . . is understood as life in Gemeinschaft (community). Gesellschaft (society) is public life—it is the world itself. In Gemeinschaft with one's family, one lives from birth on, bound to it in weal and woe. One goes into Gesellschaft as one goes into a strange country. . . . [H]uman Gesellschaft is conceived as mere coexistence of people independent of each other. . . . Gemeinschaft . . . is the lasting and genuine form of living together. In contrast to Gemeinschaft, Gesellschaft is transitory and superficial. Accordingly, Gemeinschaft should be understood as a living organism, Gesellschaft as a mechanical aggregate and artifact.

It is noteworthy that Tönnies, like many of his predecessors, drew heavily for his conception from the European experience, rather than from a contrast between European and non-European societies. In their commentary on Tönnies, the editors of his work (Loomis and McKinney, in Tönnies [1887] 1957) say,

It would be a mistake to assume that the roots of *Gemeinschaft und Gesellschaft* had no foundation other than the literature with which the author was familiar. They ran deep into the subsoil of Tönnies' own experience and observation. As a son of a well-to-do peasant family, he saw the influence of rationalism as the old rural culture of his native province, Schleswig-Holstein, had to submit to the inroads of mechanization and commercialization. Furthermore, his oldest brother was engaged in trading with English merchants so that he had, while very young, firsthand contact with two worlds—the world of the peasant rooted to his soil and the world of the merchant whose soul is in the profits of his trade.

Because of their direct knowledge of the transformation of European society, seen both in developments over time and in the evolving contrast between rural and urban areas, and between peripheral and central regions, all of these students of social evolution and founders of both anthropology and sociology could be said to have engaged in participant observation, not among distant and apparently exotic peoples as later became common for anthropologists, but in their own societies and cultures, and based their theories largely on what they had observed.

Emile Durkheim, in *The Division of Labor in Society* ([1893] 1933), framed cultural evolution in terms of the move from mechanical solidarity, in which similar segmentary groups in small-scale society were held together by their cultural commonalities, social norms were highly restrictive, and social control was dominated by criminal law and supernatural sanctions, to organic solidarity (using the term "organic" in quite a different way from Tönnies), in which a division of labor among social groups led to a high degree of interdependence, in which social norms were less restrictive and social control was based on contractual civil law and depended little on reference to supernatural forces.

Max Weber ([1925] 1947) examined, among many other developments, the increase in **rationality** in the organization and culture of European society. The two main aspects of rationality in Weber's view were, one, the declining authority of tradition and the insistence of examining beliefs and practices according to **universalistic standards**, and, two, the reorganization of rules of behavior in terms of a general, rational framework, so that individual acts are no longer good or bad in themselves but must be weighed according to their overall consequences. Weber's influential examination of *The Protestant Ethic and the Spirit of Capitalism* ([1904–1905] 1930), which explained the development of capitalist rationality as an inadvertent consequence of Protestant beliefs and comportment, illustrates through a major case study this important, evolutionary development.

RECENT AND CONTEMPORARY EVOLUTIONARY THOUGHT: ARCHAEOLOGISTS

Cultural evolution is a basic paradigm among anthropological archaeologists studying human prehistory. Examination of the long sweep of human history convinces most scholars of the validity of an evolutionary scheme of development. In his widely used textbook, Fagan (1999:234; see also Trigger 1998) makes the point clearly:

> If there is a general trend over time, it is toward increasing social and political complexity.
> Furthermore, this trend toward greater complexity has manifest itself in remarkably similar ways in terms of political and social organization.

Fagan (1999:234, emphasis in original) distinguishes between the relatively simple prestate societies, subcategorized into bands, tribes, and chiefdoms, in order of increasing complexity, and state-organized societies, which he identifies as civilizations.

> **Prestate societies** are small-scale societies based on the community, band or village. . . .
> **Bands** are autonomous and self-sufficient groups that usually consist of only a few families. They are egalitarian, with leadership coming from experience and the personal qualities of particular individuals rather than from inherited or acquired political power.
> **Tribes** are egalitarian like bands, but with more social and cultural organizations. . . .
> **Chiefdoms** are societies headed by individuals with unusual ritual, political, or entrepreneurial skills. . . . Society is still kin based, but is more hierarchical, with power concentrated in the hands of powerful kin leaders responsible for the redistribution of resources. Chiefdoms tend to have higher population densities and to display signs of social ranking. . . .
> **State-organized societies** (*civilizations*) operate on a large scale, with centralized social and political organizations, class stratification, and intensive agriculture.

Fagan (1999:240) sums up by saying that

> Archaeologists define several broad levels of sociocultural evolution in prehistory, which provide a general framework for tracing human organization through time.

Although this framework is very close to that of the mid-nineteenth-century theorists, anthropological evolutionists commonly assert that their position is very different. For example, Fagan (1999:14) says that the nineteenth-century theory proposed **unilinear**

cultural evolution, a "simplistic hypothesis" that has been "long discredited." This (alleged) old fashioned and discredited view has been replaced, according to Fagan (1999:247), by **multilinear evolution**, which "recognizes that there are many evolutionary tracks, . . ." However, if we scrutinize this distinction between unilinear and multilinear closely, it does not appear to describe accurately either the difference between nineteenth- and twentieth-century evolutionary views or even distinct theoretical positions.

All students of human cultural history must agree that there has been a unilinear evolution at the overall, general level, "toward greater complexity" as Fagan (1999:234) put it. No one imagines that the first human beings organized state societies and literary civilizations, which then universally evolved into small hunting bands. Everyone agrees that over the tens of thousands of years of cultural evolution, bands came first, more complex tribes and chiefdoms later, and states and civilizations subsequently. However, this general sequence does not necessarily hold in the specific histories of particular societies, which, depending upon local circumstances and pressures, can form at almost any level of organization and evolve into more complex or devolve into less complex forms. This was known also to the nineteenth-century theorists. Although Fagan (1999:15) claims that Morgan, for example, outlined "seven periods of human progress," Morgan ([1877] 1996) made very clear that he was speaking about "conditions," not periods. In sum, both nineteenth- and twentieth-century evolutionary theorists recognize an overall trend at the general level and a multiplicity of forms and trajectories at the specific level of individual societies and cultures. The distinction between the **general evolution** of human culture at large and the **specific evolution** of particular societies, developed by Marshall Sahlins (1960), expresses this clearly. Whether the evolution of any particular society must go through specific stages without skipping any to reach a higher level of complexity, a view that can be labeled "unilinear," or whether societies can move to higher levels of complexity through quite different trajectories, a view that can be labeled "multilinear," is another question.

Even if there is substantive agreement about cultural evolution between nineteenth- and twentieth-century evolutionary theorists, there are a number of other, important things that divide them. One is expression: the use by several nineteenth-century theorists of apparently pejorative and ethnocentric terms such as "savagery" and "barbarism" to designate lower levels of development, which offends our cultural relativity, inspires us to distance ourselves. A second is interest: the general categories of overall cultural evolution can tell us only a limited amount. Further knowledge must be based upon detailed studies—through archaeological excavation and related techniques—of the specific cultural histories of particular societies. A third is the use of ethnographic examples in evolutionary reconstruction: nineteenth-century theorists considered contemporary simpler societies equivalents of early societies; whereas, because contemporary simpler societies have histories as long as more complex societies, and, furthermore, unlike the earliest societies, coexist with more complex societies, this is no longer regarded as appropriate. But, perhaps not changing our view as much as we pretend, we still try to learn from such societies as types.

> Today's archaeologists would not dream of comparing Eskimo culture to that of the Cro-Magnons, but they still make extensive use of fundamental concepts developed by anthropologists working among hunter-gatherer and subsistence farming societies around the world. (Fagan 1999:38)

A fourth is a common convention of academic life: whether for reasons of ego enhancement, professional advancement, and/or obsessive attachment to minor details of one's thought, exaggerating the differences between one's views and those of one's predecessors is common.

THEORETICAL ISSUES IN
EVOLUTIONARY THOUGHT

The important theoretical questions about human cultural evolution are in fact other than these above-mentioned considerations. The first and most central is, what should be the criterion for judging whether evolution has taken place? At the very least, the idea of evolution, and its converse, **devolution**, implies directionality. What should count as moving toward a more evolved state? A variety of criteria has been suggested. Spencer ([1860] 1996) argued in favor of increase in size, complexity, and interdependence of parts, while Durkheim ([1893] 1933), elaborating on the same theme, specified a qualitative shift from mechanical to organic solidarity. Morgan ([1877] 1996) focused on technology as a criterion for evolution, while Marx and Engels ([1845–1846] 1996) emphasized the social relations of production. Another possible criterion, suggested by the egregiously sanguinary history of the twentieth century, is military capability, or, less politely, killing power: from the lowly and inefficient prehistoric wooden clubs and stone axes, up through spears and bows and arrows, to guns and bullets and artillery shells, and finally to the glory of A-bombs, H-bombs, and guided missiles; a remarkable evolution, in both efficiency and nastiness, particularly if we remember to insert the highly organized extermination camps. Other possible criteria might be human population size, which has grown ever rapidly over the last two millennia, or human longevity, which has increased markedly over the past century (in Canada, for example, from about forty-eight years in 1901 to seventy-eight years in 1997 [Beauchesne 1999]), or years of formal education, or material standard of living, as measured by consumption of goods and services. Finally, it would be equally possible to focus on qualitative criteria (although in practice somewhat more difficult to measure), such as democratic government, scientific discovery, individual freedom, or human rights.

Some criteria, such as population size, would likely show an evolution of more or less continual increase, and others, such as formal education, would illustrate an unrelenting increase. Yet other criteria such as democratic government and individual freedom would likely show a U-shaped trajectory rather than a clear evolution, with modern societies still not at the same level of democratic operation as nomadic hunting and gathering and segmentary pastoral societies. This evolutionary curve would appear to be true for the criteria of Marx and Engels; their (hypothetical) evolution to communism is really a return to the collective life of tribal society. Furthermore, many of the factors mentioned above as possible criteria of evolution are correlated with one another to some degree; others are not. Thus evolution according to one criterion, such as technological advancement, can be negatively correlated with other criteria, such as democratic government or individual freedom. For example, in preindustrial societies with technologically advanced systems of crop production, such as large-scale irrigation and/or terracing, social arrangements are rigid and rule is despotic, with little democracy and individual freedom. What evolution means therefore depends upon which criterion we pick.

The second important theoretical consideration in theories of evolution is what the mechanisms, or natural processes, are that lead to evolution. Is there some kind of **natural selection** at work, some type of pressure ensuring cultural evolution? Not all theorists specify such a mechanism, but some do. Marx and Engels ([1845–1846] 1996:61–63) identify contradictions between the established and institutionalized social relations of production and ownership, on the one hand, and the expanding forces of production, including technology and resources, on the other, as the driving forces of social and cultural change.

> ... [T]hese three moments, the forces of production, the state of society, and consciousness, can and must come into contradiction with one another, because the *division of labour* implies the possibility, nay the fact that intellectual and material activity—enjoyment and labour, production and consumption—devolve on different individuals ... (Marx and Engels ([1845–1846] 1996:63, emphasis in original)

The consequence of this contradiction is the class struggle for mastery. When an upcoming class—the landowners, or the middle class, or the workers—succeeds in taking power, society is remade in the image of that class's interests. Each step of expanding forces of production and social reformation is, for Marx and Engels, an evolutionary advance toward the final stage, communism.

Another formulation of the mechanism of transformation focuses less on internal dynamics and more on external relations. This is an historically serious version of "keeping up with the Joneses," identifying the pressure of neighboring societies as a force leading to evolutionary development. The argument (Fried 1975; Price 1978) is that the desire for control of resources and for independence leads societies to try to maintain their competitiveness with neighboring societies. When a society faces neighboring societies that are at a higher level of organization, which makes them stronger, there is great pressure on that society to emulate its neighbors and take on a higher level of organization. As Price (1978:181) puts it,

> . . . [W]hen the conditions of contact involve direct competition for the same resource base (exploited similarly or differently), the higher-energy system will displace the lower-energy one, by competitive exclusion. In illustration, when hunter-gatherers and cultivators compete for lands capable of supporting either mode of production, the cultivators usually push back the hunter-gatherers. State-organized polities have consistently since 3000 B.C. expanded at the expense of non-state-organized groups.

For example, if a society of small, independent bands is near a tribal society of local groups united into a regional political entity, the band society will be under threat of loss of their natural resources or their liberty should the tribal society expand as its population increases and as it seeks to improve its situation. There are three possibilities for the band society. It can retreat from the advance of the tribal society, but at the expense of leaving rich areas for marginal ones; it can let the tribal society incorporate it as an underclass, which opens its members to economic exploitation and cultural humiliation and leads to an evolution of the tribal society into a stratified one; or, it can draw its bands together and unite in a tribal structure, thus (in certain senses) evolving by duplicating the more complex structure of its neighbors. The exact same scenario holds for tribal societies with state societies for neighbors. That is why tribal societies that exist today are located in remote deserts and mountains, just as band societies that exist today are located in deserts and forests.

Our third, and final, consideration of theoretical import is whether evolution can be considered progress. This is quite clearly a value judgment, on which people might disagree. But to nineteenth-century observers of the changes in western Europe, there was no doubt that over the last centuries things had gotten much, much better. When they looked around the world, it was clear to them that plenty was better than scarcity; wealth better than poverty; that machines made work light, and that was a good thing; that science worked better than magic; that vast libraries were richer than oral tales; that large universities were wellsprings of new discoveries; that great cities had more to offer than small villages; that law was better than vendetta; that representative parliaments were better than chiefs and kings; that Beethoven symphonies were better than impromptu songs; and that, just as the present was better than the past, with intelligent effort, the future could be better than the present. While most readers of this book will be less impressed than nineteenth-century evolutionists with the plenty of foodstuffs, the universal use of electricity, the inexpensive availability of manufactured goods, the ease and speed of mechanized transportation, and the curing power of modern medicine, this is not because we would not feel their absence greatly, but because we take them for granted. (When we, gentle readers, find ourselves in a situation requiring that we use outdoor toilet facilities instead of indoor plumbing, wash clothes by hand in cold water, and walk to get from place to place, our minds tend to focus rapidly on the marvels of modern conveniences.) Nonetheless, the idea of progress is deeply imbedded in our Western cultural psyches, and we look to the future always with the hope and expectation that things can be improved.

What we count as improvement might vary from group to group and individual to individual, and our concerns at the beginning of the twenty-first century will inevitably be at least somewhat different from those of nineteenth-century commentators. For example, the increasing "conquest of nature" and the effective exploitation of natural resources were clear signs of progress to nineteenth-century observers. But now, for many of us, after so much of our environment has been devastated or destroyed by human interference, an increasing respect for nature and ability to live in harmony with other species would be regarded as progress. In the field of social relations, while in the nineteenth century attention was given to the rule of law and to formal political rights, many of us today would gauge progress in the degree of equality or in the implementation of human rights. Other developments seen so clearly in the twentieth century, such as the extraordinary increase in power of destructive weaponry and the increasingly efficient application of totalitarian techniques of political control, are certainly evolution of a sort, but not many of us would care to be the kind of people who would regard these as progress.

NEO-EVOLUTIONISM: ENERGY RULES!

In twentieth-century anthropology, the focus of evolutionary theorists has been less the evaluative question of evolutionary progress than the understanding of evolution as cumulative social and cultural transformation over time. The historical facts of the specific historical evolution of particular societies are so diverse, that some anthropologists have sought critical, underlying or common factors that run through the many different forms. In mid-century, Leslie White (1959; [1943] 1996) identified what he thought was the critical factor: energy. He argued that, as part of nature, human beings had to expend energy to gain the necessities of life. The more energy that was captured by people, the more there was to serve their needs. Technological innovations can be seen as ways of capturing more energy to work for human beings. Beginning with human muscle power, domestication captured energy from plants and animals to work for people, water- and fire-driven machines captured more energy, fossil-fuel-driven machines captured yet more, and nuclear energy ever more. According to White, social and cultural systems reflect the amount of energy at their disposal. This is how White (1959:144–45, emphasis in original) states his materialist thesis:

> Social systems are but the social form of expression of technological control over the forces of nature. Social evolution is therefore a function of technological development. Social systems evolve as the amount of energy harnessed per capita per year increases, other factors remaining constant. That is to say, they become more differentiated structurally, more specialized functionally, and as a consequence of differentiation and specialization, special mechanisms of integration and regulation are developed. Thus human social evolution becomes intelligible in terms of entropy, in terms of a corollary of the second law of thermodynamics: *the degree of organization of a system is proportional to the concentration of energy within the system.*

White (1959:ch. 12) illustrates with the agricultural revolution. After some million years of hunting and gathering by small, scattered groups with simple forms of organization, the beginning of agriculture and raising of livestock caused astonishingly rapid development. These included, according to V. Gordon Childe (1951, cited in White 1959:369),

> artificial irrigation using canals and ditches; the plow; the harnessing of animal motive-power; the sailboat; wheeled vehicles; orchard-husbandry; fermentation; the production and use of copper; bricks; the arch; glazing; the seal; and . . . a solar calendar, writing, numeral notation, and bronze.

What was the social result of these innovations? White (1959:369) argues that

> It took only three or four thousand years to transform primitive tribal systems, activated by human energy and subsisting upon wild foods, into great urban cultures sustained by the intensive cul-

tivation of cereals. But with the achievement of the great urban, literate, metallurgical, calendrical cultures, the curve of cultural development leveled off. . . .

Further social and cultural evolution would await new technology to capture significantly greater amounts of energy.

CONTEMPORARY EVOLUTIONISM 1: COGNITION RULES!

In a letter to the (Canadian) *National Post* (1 Jan. 2000:B9), Ruben F. W. Nelson sums up his view of human history:

> Until now, every human being has lived within one of three cosmic [read: cultural] stories. First are the stories of tribal peoples. Up until 8,000 years ago, east, west, north, south, all persons were tribal. Second are the stories of tradition-oriented civilizations, which ruled all but the remotest parts of this planet from 4000 BC to 1700 AD. The third story is the one Canadians [and Americans, Europeans, Japanese, and other Asian Tigers] know so well—the story of industrial societies.

This outline is widely accepted by anthropologists. The exact number of stages and the labels used might differ somewhat. Service (1971:157) distinguishes three preindustrial types that represent evolutionary stages:

> (1) the Egalitarian Society, out of which grew (2) the Hierarchical Society, which was replaced in only a few instances in the world by the Empire-State that was the basis of the next stage (3) the Archaic Civilization or Classical Empire.

For Ernest Gellner (1988:16 and passim) there are three stages in all, cultural development being associated with the ecological stage:

> Mankind has passed through three fundamental stages: (1) hunting/gathering; (2) agrarian society; (3) industry society.

In spite of the differences in number of stages and labels, which are significant but secondary, there is considerable agreement among anthropologists on the course of general evolution, together with the understanding that the trajectories of development of individual societies are another matter.

The main question, however, remains open. What is the import of the course of general evolution? For White, as we have seen, it is a record of, and testimony to, the determining effect of control over energy. For Gellner (1988), the different ecological stages reflect different kinds of institutionalized cognition, of the aims and procedures of knowledge.

Gellner (1988:60–61) begins with the argument that cultural knowledge can do two quite distinct things: it can integrate social life, the world, and the universe into a coherent story that promotes and rationalizes social solidarity; or it can measure, in a disinterested fashion, hard, cold, external reality. What presents such a serious problem for people is that cultural knowledge cannot effectively do both of these at the same time:

> ... [O]ne may in fact formulate a supremely important if rough law
> of the intellectual history of mankind: *logical and social coherence
> are inversely related.* The more you have of one, the less you can
> hope to have of the other. (Gellner 1988:61, emphasis in original)

There is always social pressure for the culturally instituted ideas about the universe, the world, human nature, health, wealth, and happiness to fit with and support established social relationships and their rules and norms.

In small, hunting-and-gathering societies, largely local in focus, cultural knowledge is heavily norm-loaded and ritually inculcated. For example, the absence of game important for hunting might be attributed to someone having broken the norm of incest or having hidden rather than shared food. Or someone's illness might be attributed to someone else's anger and its wounding power. Correction of these violations would likely take a ritual form of cleansing the fault and redressing the balance between people and nature. The degree of referential (objective) knowledge about the causes of scarcity of game, strictly based on assessment of external factors, would be limited and fragmented (Gellner 1988:51).

Agrarian society, based upon domestication and agriculture and the storage of food, has a regional scope, and socially features a division of labor, with a hierarchical elite and a class of religious specialists. While the elite directs its attention to the use of coercion, for both extracting surpluses from the cultivating masses and defending its realm against external attack, religious leaders are busy legitimizing and justifying instituted social arrangements. The emphasis shifts "from norm-loaded, ritually inculcated concepts to explicit affirmations and injunctions, welded into a mutually supporting structure" (Gellner 1988:74). Writing is put to the use of setting down a clear and general framework of knowledge. But, once again, and even more so, the knowledge is socially oriented.

> Knowledge is equated with the reverent apprehension of morally
> binding norms. ... The Ideas stand in moral judgment over facts;
> facts do not ... stand in cognitive judgment over Ideas. ...
>
> The system is designed to serve primarily *one* purpose, the pro-
> vision of a unified charter of a social order and its vision. (Gellner
> 1988:75)

In such schemes, God or the gods have sanctified the social and political order. If you avoid your duty and do not give your labor or pay your taxes, you will go to hell and suffer excruciating tortures throughout eternity. (It almost makes paying taxes sound attractive.) If you rebel against God's anointed ruler, then, the king's men, on behalf of God, will strike you dead. And then you will go to hell. If you disagree with these rules and beliefs, you are a heretic, and we will burn you, and then you will go to hell to be burned through all eternity. Or, to take another religious framework, you are a servant because it is your destiny based upon what you did in your previous life. But if you devote yourself to your duty as a servant, you will be rewarded by being born in a higher status in your next life. If, on the other hand, you do not do your duty in this life, in your next life you will be born a dog or a cockroach. In these socially oriented visions driven by the need to legitimize established social relations, there is not much functional knowledge about the external world. In truth, agrarian society was not really very nice. As Gellner (1988:269) says, "the traditional state was seldom much good at anything, really, other than killing people and taking away their surplus."

Modern industrial and postindustrial society was not so much based on any particular invention, such as the steam engine or mass production. Rather it was established on

> the generic or second-order discovery that successful systematic investigation of Nature, and the application of the findings for the purpose of increased output, are feasible, and, once initiated, not too difficult. (Gellner 1988:17–18)

Industrial society is based upon a revolutionary shift in the orientation of culturally instituted knowledge. Referential knowledge, based upon empirical fact, becomes the dominant paradigm. For the first time, there is

> a culture which no longer accepts its own concepts as ordained from on high, but which chooses its own, and endows them with only a conditional authority. . . . External nature and the social order are now [understood to be] mutually independent, . . . The independence and externality of natural truth is [now understood to be] the complement of the human foundation of all authority. (Gellner 1988:126)

Without this revolution in culture, industrial society would not have been possible. Once this revolution in culture takes place, it leads to "unparalleled economic and military power, incomparably greater than that ever granted to other civilizations, to other visions" (Gellner 1988:200). And in the end, all other cultures will be absorbed.

In the fifteen years or so since Gellner wrote his book, there have been several startling developments. As Gellner (1988) discussed the conflict between democratic and communist industrial regimes, the fall of communism would be of great interest to him. All I have space to say here is that the fall of communism has led to increasing uniformity in global political and economic culture. The second development is economic globalization, including the increase in unimpeded trade, the expansion of international corporations, and the strengthening of international regulatory agencies. The result is that various parts of the world are increasingly interdependent, and the entire world is becoming the effective operating unit. The third development is the globalization of communications, with satellites broadcasting around the world and the Internet connecting people and corporations around the world. The result of these developments, all based upon industrial technology, is that the effective operating system is increasingly the entire globe. This appears to validate Gellner's observation that culture based upon referential cognition is bound to spread and triumph over other cultures. It also appears to satisfy the general criteria for social and cultural evolution of increased size and complexity. If this is correct, we are not just speculating about cultural evolution, we are experiencing it directly.

CONTEMPORARY EVOLUTIONISM 2:
NATURAL SELECTION RULES!

According to modern biological theory, evolution is a result of natural selection, originally posited by Darwin, and genetic inheritance, discovered by Mendel. Thus all animal species have evolved through the history of the earth by means of five processes: (1) inheritance, the passing of genes from parents to children; (2) mutation, random variation of genes; (3) drift, the shifting of the genetic profile in a population; (4) gene flow (or lack of it due to isolation) between populations; and (5) natural selection, the effects of the environment on relative success of members of a population (Irons 1979b:5). But of these processes, natural selection is the dominant force in determining the specific characteristics of organisms.

If the evolution of all animal species and animal behavior is explained by genetic inheritance and natural selection, would this not be true of human beings, and should not investigation of these same processes among human beings explain a great deal about the human behavior, society, and culture? These are the questions posed by anthropologists drawing on theories of **sociobiology**, the subfield of biology that studies evolutionary processes that influence social behavior. This field of study within anthropology was originally labeled sociobiology but has latterly been called **evolutionary ecology** or **behavioral ecology**.

The basic argument of evolutionary ecology is that "[h]uman beings, like other organisms, are products of natural selection" (Irons

1979b:4). This means that human nature and the commonalities of all human beings, such as the ability to learn and the capacity to adjust to environmental conditions, are the result of natural selection. Similarly, differences among human beings, such as social organization and culture, are the result of adaptations to different environments. Adaptation is understood in the strict biological sense of "maximization of genetic representation in future generations," also called "maximization of inclusive fitness" (Irons 1979a:xii). That is, evolutionary success is measured by the genetic variant with the greater number of offspring. Thus, if those individuals with greater size, sharing, strength, calmness, speed, intelligence, hair, cooperativeness, aggressiveness, hearing, or sight produce more children that themselves successfully reproduce, than individuals with other characteristics, they are better adapted and more successful in evolutionary terms. The reason for this is that the successful characteristics are more suitable for the environmental conditions in which the people live. Natural selection is the process by which those best adapted to their environment reproduce more effectively than others and are represented in greater numbers in succeeding generations, eventually replacing those less adapted with fewer offspring and thus transforming their genetic population into mirrors of themselves.

For example, among the Central Asian Turkmen of northeastern Iran (Irons 1975, 1979c; see also Chagnon 1979), some individuals in the population end up having more descendants in the generation following them than do other individuals, and those who have more descendants have (by definition) a higher level of **Darwinian fitness**. What is the reason for these different rates? One difference is wealth. Irons (1979c) compares the wealthier half of the population with the poorer half, and finds that, in examining mortality, on average the poorer die younger and the wealthier live longer, and that, in examining fertility, on average the wealthier have more children. Turkmen men in the wealthier half of the population have on average 4.42 sons and 3.71 daughters, whereas men in the poor half have on average 2.39 sons and 2.25 daughters (Irons 1979c:Table 10-5). So the genes of wealthier men are increasingly represented in following generations.

Why does greater wealth lead to higher reproductive success among the Yomut Turkmen? Among this nomadic, tribal people, individuals raise livestock and grow grain to feed themselves and their families. Their degree of success in production determines their standard of living. Individuals in wealthier families succeed in contributing more descendants to the following generations because of their better standard of living (Irons 1979c:267–68):

> Wealthier individuals of both sexes enjoy better diets and medical care and devote less time to forms of labor which are strenuous or involve high risks. This in turn affects survivorship rates. Wealth-

ier males have higher fertility because their families can afford to acquire brides for them at an earlier-than-average age, because they remarry more quickly after a wife dies, and because they are more frequently polygynous. Polygyny among the Turkmen is a rich man's luxury. The bridewealth necessary to acquire a second or third wife is three times what one must pay for a first wife.

However, differences in wealth among the Turkmen are not just differences in inherited position and resources. Because the Turkmen are an egalitarian people admitting no status differences amongst themselves, and because wealth among the Turkmen is highly volatile (Irons 1994), economic success is in the long run the result of effort and ability. Turkmen culture lauds wealth as a primary goal of success, and Turkmen strive for it. Perhaps, then (and here I am going beyond what Irons says explicitly), among the Turkmen success in gaining wealth is a reflection of personal qualities—such as astuteness, patience, tenacity—which are based in genes and which are then passed on to the next generation in greater numbers. If so, natural selection, choosing and passing on in greater numbers those genes underlying qualities of success, is constantly improving the population.

Irons (1979c:258) argues that striving for wealth among the Turkmen is not strictly an individual phenomenon. Rather, Turkmen culture institutes wealth as a value and defines wealth as a major criterion of success. Turkmen individuals are thus led toward biological success by their culture. Nor is this unique to the Turkmen. Irons (1979c:258) says,

I suggest as a hypothesis that in most human societies cultural success consists in accomplishing those things which make biological success (that is, a high inclusive fitness) probable. While cultural success is by definition something people are conscious of, they may often be unaware of the biological consequences of their behavior.

This argument follows from the more general one (Irons 1979c:258) that

Human beings track their environments and behave in ways, which, given the specific environment in which they find themselves, maximize inclusive fitness; what is observed as culture and social structure is the outcome of this process.

So culture and social organization are, in this theoretical perspective, themselves adapted to the natural and social environmental conditions. And culture and social organization serve as guides, leading people to follow them to reproductive success and Darwinian fitness.

While in this Darwinian-Mendelian perspective individuals must be selfish in a genetic sense, people can advance their individual interests by entering into social relations and cooperating, even sacrificing for others. Evolutionary ecology conceptualizes this as **reciprocal altruism** (Irons 1979b:22):

> Altruistic behavior can be favored by natural selection if there is a
> high probability that the organism assisted by this behavior will
> eventually reciprocate with altruistic behavior toward the original
> altruist. . . . By definition, such behavior is favored by natural se-
> lection only if the final effect for the altruist is an increase in its
> own genetic material in descending generations.

By cooperating together—as in forming a production group to do things
that an individual could not do (such as clearing forest or building an
irrigation system), or a defense group to protect themselves against
predators—individuals increase the likelihood of their own survival
and well-being and thus reproduction. However, there is always the risk
of some people trying to benefit from others' altruism without recipro-
cating, thus improving their own position in comparison to others. For
this too natural selection has an answer (Irons 1979b:24): Such well-
entrenched human traits as "moral outrage, the bearing of grudges, and
even the satisfying quality of vengeance are all adaptive responses to
the reciprocal altruist's problem of dealing with non-reciprocators."

WHY DO HUNTERS AND GATHERERS WORK?

How can we explain why hunters hunt and gatherers gather? This
is one question among many about hunters and gatherers addressed by
anthropological evolutionary ecologists (Kelly 1995). Hawkes (1993)
argues that the obvious answers are not always correct. This is because
some kinds of food, mainly large game kills, are "public goods," shared
among many people in hunting-and-gathering groups, while other
types, mainly food that is gathered, are not. What motivates hunters to
hunt, asks Hawkes, when they must give away their food?

Among tropical hunters and gatherers, gathering brings in more
food than hunting. Women mainly gather, and provide their families
with food. Men do gather some, and can provide their families and themselves with the proceeds, but they often hunt, even though it is a less efficient way of bringing in calories and even though the proceeds will be
spread thinly among all camp members, with themselves and their families getting little of the proceeds. Why do men invest their time and
energy in a less efficient means of bringing in food and why do they
choose to bring in proceeds that must be distributed to everyone, instead
of those that would be exclusively used for their families and themselves?

A favorite explanation in anthropology for the sharing of hunting
proceeds is that success in hunting is chancy and the income for any
individual highly variable over time. Therefore, he who brings in game
shares it now so that he can receive game food from others when he
misses and they hit. Sharing is thus seen as a kind of security arrange-

ment, an insurance pact (Lee 1993:60 and passim). Evolutionary ecologist Hawkes (1993:345) rejects this explanation on the grounds that the ethnographic evidence shows that certain individual hunters consistently bring in most of the meat, and others consistently bring in little or nothing. So in reality a few good hunters provide most or all of the meat, and a number of nonhunters share the proceeds.

So why do hunters hunt? Why do they not gather and feed their families? And why do they continue to give meat to nonproducing males and their families? Hawkes (1993:349) has an hypothesis:

> Foragers do better to choose neighbors who provide collective goods. If there are advantages to being preferred as a neighbor, individuals can gain them by trading off the consumption advantages from targeting private good and supplying collective goods instead. Advantages may include deference in decisions about travel, support in disputes . . ., and enhanced mating opportunities. Preferences in association will be likely to have fitness consequences [i.e., in more offspring].

In other words, if a hunter provides food, the men who receive the food will give him deference and political support, and the women will favor him with greater sexual access and the higher possibility of offspring. Does this political support and sexual access lead to a higher level of fitness for successful hunters? According to Hawkes (1993:351), evidence from some hunting populations indicates a positive correlation between hunting success and reproductive success, a finding consistent with her hypothesis.

Strategies for reproductive success vary by sex. Females invest heavily in the limited number of children they are able to produce, while males attempt to father as many children as possible. This difference is reflected in reproductive strategies of hunters and gatherers. Females gather and use the proceeds to support themselves and their children. Men hunt and share the proceeds with everyone. As Hawkes (1993:350) frames it,

> Family nutrition as compared with alliance and mating advantages will often give different relative fitness payoffs by sex because of the same fundamental asymmetries that lead women to invest more in child care than do men.

In short, women use their resources to support families, while men use their resources to chase skirts. (Hawkes's analysis could also be read as having a feminist subtext that contrasts the constructive role of women in supporting their children, with the tendency of men to devote themselves to seeking social prestige and extrafamilial sexual favors.)

Are women gatherers, then, left on their own to support their children, rather like single parents today? In one respect, yes, according to Hawkes, O'Connell, and Jones (1997:562); men are not contributing:

... [M]en's foraging choices are often inconsistent with family provisioning. ... [H]unting cannot cover the day-to-day nutritional requirements of weaned offspring among contemporary savanna
foragers [i.e., hunters and gatherers] and seems even less likely to
have done so in the distant past. The assumption that nuclear families are fundamental *economic* units among modern human foragers, let alone ancestral hominids, is due for revision.

But mothers can count on other women, *"matrilineally related
females"* (Hawkes et al. 1997:561), especially their own mothers, who
contribute the proceeds of gathering to their grandchildren and help to
maintain their nourishment after the children have been weaned and
are no longer receiving their mother's milk. Among one hunting and
gathering people, the Hadza, *"no nursing woman lacks a postmenopausal* [female] *helper"* (Hawkes et al. 1997:563). In helping to nourish
their grandchildren, these postmenopausal women are advancing their
own Darwinian fitness by ensuring that their genes, passed through
their daughters, make their way safely down through the next generation. As a result of these relations and contributions, "the family" as a
social and economic unit among hunters and gatherers appears to be
an all-female, multigenerational unit, with men separate, using their
resources to pursue their social and reproductive interests.

Chapter Seven

Critical Advocacy
Feminism and Postmodernism

To ask about feminist theory is to misunderstand the thrust of feminism, according to the advice of a distinguished feminist anthropologist (personal communication). Feminism, she said, is not a theory; it is a political movement. Arising from what was called the women's movement in the 1960s, feminism has always aimed at social and cultural change. As Ortner (1974:67; see also Slocum [1975] 2000) puts it,

> My interest in the problem [of women's status] is of course more than academic: I wish to see genuine change come about, the emergence of a social and cultural order in which as much of the range of human potential is open to women as to men. The universality of female subordination, the fact that it exists within every type of social and economic arrangement and in societies of every degree of complexity, indicates to me that we are up against something very profound, very stubborn. . . .

The evolution of feminist anthropology has gone hand in hand with feminist politics. But asserted common interests do not guarantee agreement on strategy, tactics, or even goals, and certainly not on theory. There are within the broad movement of feminism a number of different theories, some complementary and some conflicting. Let us explore several of the main themes and the various positions taken by feminist anthropologists.

Ortner (1974:67–69) argues, as an empirical generalization, "the universality of female subordination," that women in all societies have "second-class status." Ortner is focusing here especially on the cultural level, on the level of explicit ideology, and the way that this victimizes and disadvantages women by construing them as inferior to men. She (1974:69) recognizes that

> Observable on-the-ground details of women's activities, contribu-
> tions, powers, influence, etc., [are] often at variance with cultural
> ideology. . . . This is the level of direct observation, often adopted
> now by feminist-oriented anthropologists.

But these practical variants do exist, according to Ortner, within a subordinate cultural evaluation of women. Ortner's question is, what
accounts for this negative evaluation of women? Ortner's (1974:73)
answer, which draws for theoretical inspiration from Lévi-Strauss's
structuralism, has two parts: First, "culture (i.e., every culture) . . .
asserts itself to be not only distinct from but superior to nature." Second, "culture (still equated relatively unambiguously with men) . . .
sees [women] as being more rooted in, or having more direct affinity
with, nature." Ortner (1974:73–74, 83) argues that this cultural conception of women is based on woman's bodily functions, which are construed as closer to nature, and woman's social roles, which are at a
lower order of cultural process than man's. In consequence, woman is
believed to have a psychic structure closer to nature.

FEMALE POWER

Rogers (1975) grants that "the myth of male dominance" is widespread, not only among feminist anthropologists, but also in societies
around the world. But she (1975:729) argues that we should not take it
at face value: "the 'myth' of male dominance does not directly determine
ordinary behavior: males do not actually dominate, nor do either males
or females literally believe them to be dominant." In peasant communities, such as those Rogers (1975:729) reviews and the one in northeastern France in which she carried out her own ethnographic research,

> women control at least the major portion of important resources
> and decisions. In other words, if we limit our investigation to the
> relative actual power of peasant men and women, eliminating for
> the moment those sources of power from the outside world which
> are beyond the reach of peasant men or women, women appear to
> be generally more powerful.

The myth of male dominance gives peasant men a sense of high
standing, even though for a variety of practical reasons their power is
minimal. Those reasons include the monopoly of politics by the state
and its agents, the spatial and social dispersion of men and their com-
plete investment in primary production, and the functioning of the
household and its members, female and male alike, as the production
unit. In practice, women bring property of their own into their marriage, and in the household economy that is the basis of village life, hold

the household money and make the family budget, handle much of the selling and buying, and so control the family's economic resources. They are part of a close and cooperating family network of women, and as well part of interhousehold groups and networks of women "heavily influencing community public opinion and mediating between groups of men. . . . It is village women, not men, who are the key actors in those informal structures to which peasants have access" (Rogers 1975:735–36; for a Mediterranean peasant community similar in gender relations, see Salzman 1999:ch. 3). So the myth of male dominance stands, but the reality is different. According to Rogers (1975:729),

> The perpetuation of this "myth" is in the interests of both peasant women and men, because it gives the latter [i.e., men] the *appearance* of power and control over all sectors of village life, while at the same time giving to the former [i.e., women] *actual* power over those sectors of life in the community which may be controlled by villagers. The two sex groups, in effect, operate within partially divergent systems of perceived advantages, values, and prestige, so that the members of each group see themselves as the "winners" in respect to the other. Neither men nor women believe that the "myth" is an accurate reflection of the actual situation. However, each sex group believes (or appears to believe, so avoiding confrontation) that the opposite sex perceives the myth as reality, with the result that each is actively engaged in maintaining the illusion that males are, in fact, dominant.

Rogers thus attempts to explain the idea of male supremacy, while demonstrating the reality of female power. Women in peasant societies are shown to be not under control, but in control; not isolated, but united; not subordinate, but influential; not submissive, but powerful; not weak, but strong.

The importance of women is seen not only in peasant societies, but also in nonstate indigenous societies. In much of Africa, Asia, and the Pacific, primary production in the form of subsistence hoe farming was the sphere of women. Bossen (1975:592) concludes that "the productivity of women [in hoe-farming regions] was at least equal to, if not greater than, that of men." And it was not just that women were given a lot of work to do; rather, particularly in Africa, women's income and property rights were independently held. Furthermore, in West Africa, parts of the Caribbean, Latin America, and Southeast Asia, women were traditionally active traders (Bossen 1975:593). According to Leacock ([1983] 2000; cp. commentators' comments following Leacock 1978; Van Kirk 1987), in all communally organized societies, which included many foraging and horticultural societies around the world, men and women fully participated in primary production and had egalitarian relations. In many North American native societies, women were family heads and political councilors and representatives. Bossen

(1975:594) argues similarly about Navajo women and their traditional roles. But if this is true, what is the origin of gender hierarchy and the subordination of women?

Leacock ([1983] 2000) argues that gender hierarchy in previously egalitarian North American Indian societies resulted from contact with Europeans and from the transformation of economies to market orientation and the reorientation of politics to dealing with Europeans. Bossen (1975) makes a parallel argument about "development," the shift in local communities from subsistence to market production and from local control of knowledge and politics to supralocal organization and decision making. What happens is that "women are excluded from productive roles in the modern sector and phased out of traditional productive roles as part of the process of 'development'" (Bossen 1975:593), a view supported also by her research in a Guatemalan town. Bossen (1975:594–95) concludes,

> [M]odernization or economic "development" . . . exerts strong pressures to reduce or limit the traditional productive activities of women and severely restricts or prohibits their entry into modern productive occupations. . . . [M]odernization does not increase sexual equality, productivity, or independence for women, but rather . . . produces modern inequality, the devaluation of female labor, and economic dependence—in a word, "underdevelopment."

Thus for Bossen and Leacock, gender inequality is not universal or inevitable, but is the specific historical result of external interference and capitalist economies on other, more egalitarian, societies.

As we have seen in these examples, feminist anthropologists, while pursuing the political project of advancing the cause of women through demonstrating both the victimization and maltreatment of women and the importance and value of women, have drawn on and been inspired by various theoretical orientations. Ortner (1974) drew on Lévi-Straussian structuralism, while Rogers (1975) applied functionalist analysis, and Bossen (1975) and Leacock ([1983] 2000) were strongly influenced by marxist materialism. Other feminist anthropologists have applied evolutionary theory (e.g., Slocum [1975] 2000), Geertzian symbolic analysis (e.g., Boddy 1989; Delaney 1991), and Barthian generative models (e.g., Ortner 1984).

In its influence on anthropology more generally, feminist anthropology, arising largely from the interests and concerns of women researchers, contributed to anthropological theory a stronger sense of **epistemological relativism**, the doctrine that knowledge and truth, like beauty, are in the eyes of the beholder. Just as women, because of what they shared with other women, were able to see women as victims and women as heroines in a way that men researchers never did, so too each researcher is, according to epistemological relativism, constrained in perception by her or his social **position** and cultural precepts. In other words, what people see and understand depends upon the position that they are in and from which they observe. Feminists add the dimension of gender to the positioning of class identified by Marxists as determinant of perspective. The implication of epistemological relativism is that only positioned understanding is possible, and therefore there is no such thing as objective knowledge.

Feminism's epistemological relativism is held in various degrees by various feminist researchers. Some accept the moderate view that position influences one's understanding, making some things easier to see and other things more difficult, but that with care and collaboration it is possible to work toward an objective truth. Other feminist researchers take the radical position that position determines understanding, that what is true for you depends upon your position, and consequently that what is important is whether one's truth advances the right side, advances feminism rather than patriarchy. While these differences are present in feminism, the overall effect was to advance epistemological relativism, and this became and continues to be an important influence on postmodernism.

Feminism's political commitment to women and to bettering the position of women also influenced postmodernism and postmodern anthropology. Feminism as a political project aimed at change, and success was defined in advancing the interests of women. Feminist anthropology was therefore not merely an academic subject, not a matter only of knowledge, but a crusade for change, for doing the right thing, for freedom and equality, for social and cultural morality. This political and moral position was, as we shall see, incorporated in postmodern anthropology.

PRECURSORS OF POSTMODERN SENSIBILITY

Never in Anger (1970), Jean Briggs's highly regarded report on her seventeen-month field study of the Utkuhikhalingmiut Eskimo, a group of twenty to thirty-five persons living at the mouth of Back River, northwest of Hudson Bay, focuses on the emotional life and norms of her Eskimo hosts, but also on her own. Here is a sample (1970:261–62) from the chapter, "Kapluna [Euro-American] Daughter":

> My relationship with Inuttiaq [Briggs's Eskimo "father"] must have suffered more than most. Though my irritability overflowed in other directions at times, it was he who bore the brunt of it, because of the frequency with which our wills collided. The time I objected to Inuttiaq's sitting in the open door was the first of several occasions when anger was openly recognized between us. The most memorable of these storms occurred that first January, shortly after Inut-

tiaq's return from Gjoa Haven. The two weeks of his absence had
been an especially trying period for me. Having looked forward to a
long and peaceful interlude in which to work, free from the interference of Inuttiaq's demands, I had found myself instead faced with
an iglu so frigid and a mother ["mother," her Eskimo hostess] so
passive that I could accomplish nothing at all. Silently, I fretted
and fumed over the swelling pile of penciled scrawls, which there
was no way to type. Obviously, nothing could be done until Inuttiaq
returned, but I determined that when he did come, I would take
drastic steps to improve my working conditions.

Throughout Briggs's book, she recounts encounters, discussions, and
confrontations between herself and her Eskimo hosts and informants,
and also her own reactions to these and the reactions of the Eskimo individuals, insofar as she can find them out or figure them out. In spite of
the temperature, this is no cold, objective description. Briggs's personal
relations with her Eskimo hosts were a major part of her experience in
the field and an important source of information. As she (1970:6) says,

> ... [I]n addition to describing what the Utku themselves say about
> feelings, I draw on more personal data. One the one hand I describe
> my observations of Utku behavior and the feelings that the behav-
> ior seemed to me to portray; and on the other hand I describe the
> feelings that I myself had in particular situations. My justification
> for this is that I was an intrinsic part of the research situation. The
> responses of my hosts to my actions and my feelings, and my own
> reactions to the situations in which I found myself—my empathy
> and my experience of contrasts between my feelings and those of
> my hosts—were all invaluable sources of data.

Briggs's emphasis on the ethnographic field researcher as an active
part of the research process, and her conscious and explicit use of the
researcher's interactions with and reactions to the people being studied,
marks *Never in Anger* as a precursor of the postmodern sensibility in
anthropology. So too is Briggs's sense of the status of her report, not as
an objective, scientific account, but one person's attempt to understand
other people. The one occasion that I met Briggs, in the Negev Desert
(quite a contrast to the Arctic) in the early 1980s, she said to me—char-
acterizing her view of what ethnography is—that we go to the field and
then we come back and tell our story. "Our story" is intended to indicate
personal accounts by individual observers and authors, accounts with
no strong claims to scientific precision or distanced objectivity.

Briggs was of course not alone in her emphasis on the researcher's
subjectivity and the result of research being one person's "story" of
what was seen. Geertz's (1973) emphasis on research as interpretation,
which influenced many cultural analysts, has supported the shift
toward recognizing, acknowledging, and in some cases even celebrating
subjectivity. These elements of Briggs's ethnography and Geertz's the-

ory have been taken up as tenets of postmodern anthropology, the emphasis on the subjectivity of ethnographic (or any other) account resulting from and laying bare the centrality of the researcher in determining the nature of the research finding, of the ethnographic story.

Another ethnography in a similar spirit is *The Broken Fountain* by Thomas Belmonte, who carried out research for a year in 1974–75 in a poor quarter of Naples. Belmonte (1979:x) sets out his guidelines in the preface:

> When we study human beings we risk a problematical relationship with them. As in all other human relationships, a stance of pure objectivity (eliminating the self) is as destructive to communication as is a stance of pure subjectivity (eliminating the other). If cultural anthropology ceases to rely for insight upon an ongoing dialogue in which subject and object constantly change places and reverse roles, it will become a barren technic, a dried husk. . . .

Belmonte's (1979:xi) methodology followed from this:

> The method of field research was pure participant observation . . . I learned about lower-class Neapolitans by living with them. . . . My approach was not to dig and hunt for data, in structured methodical ways, but to watch for it and wait for it, as I navigated my way through what was essentially [for Belmonte] an exotic milieu.

Belmonte's disinclination to collect systematic information was reinforced after his initial, faltering attempt (1979:43–44).

> I decided that I could at last attempt to take a brief census, a thankless task which yielded only fragmentary results. Eventually I found someone who would assist me. After obtaining repeated assurances of my good intentions, she sat down with me and enumerated the number of people in each apartment, giving their occupations, past and present. The information flowed forth effortlessly. But the next day this woman, a local housewife, informed me that I would never know the secrets of Fontana del Re:
>
> > "Did you think I could tell you the truth, Tommaso, when you asked me all those questions? I had to lie left and right! If you knew how much I had to leave out!"
> > "You mean, Signora, if you said 'housewife,' you really meant 'whore'?"
> > "Exactly, things like that."

Furthermore, for Belmonte (1979:xi), fieldwork was not oriented only to collecting information, but was an occasion of personal experience and transformation.

> Participant observation was a means to an end, but it was also an end in itself. It was an immersion in otherness, a prolonged listening, an alternation of self.

The emphasis on interpersonal **dialogue** between researchers and subjects, the deemphasis and casting aside of positive methodology and of the goal of collecting systematic information, and the orientation toward personal engagement and transformation of the self are further features of the postmodern spirit and postmodern theory.

Another feature of postmodernism is its attention to the ethnographic text, and to the process of writing as an element in constituting the ethnographic findings (Clifford and Marcus 1986; Geertz 1988). From this perspective, different authors and anthropological schools can be analyzed to exhibit (and sometimes debunk) the rhetorical devices used to establish authorial authority, convey and distort information, invoke theory, fill in blind spots, and so on. Postmodern ethnographies do not all follow the same formula, but they often privilege certain forms of presentation, one of which is the emotive impression, often in a literary style, used repeatedly by Belmonte (1979:7, emphasis in original).

> The spirit of place in Naples is the living force of the place. It is resolute and passionate, but it is also unconscious, and insensate to the prod of awareness and reason. As such it can enrage, or it becomes hypnotic. The movement in Naples . . . combine [sic] into a devastating assault on the senses. Or else the entire scene retreats, slowing and setting finally into a brilliantly colored frieze depicting a grand, if raucous, *Commedia*. . . . The tendency of the soul in Naples is toward forgetfulness, to let consciousness fall into abandon. . . .

However, even with his methodological emphasis on his own personal experience, interpersonal dialogues, and emotive impressions, and a rejection of systematic data, Belmonte (1979:143) does not shy away from general assessments and theoretical explanations.

> The Neapolitan urban poor . . . inhabit . . . a crude, loud, pushy world where the moral order is exposed as a fraud which conceals the historical ascendancy of cunning and force.
> Cunning and force, the *materia prima* of life in the poor quarters.

Nor does Belmonte (1979:102, also ch. 9) hesitate to side with the victims and identify the villains. "The brutality of the poor is learned. It imitates the brutality of class." The Neapolitan poor are the underclass, the under-proletarians, below the workers in an oppressive class system that deprives them of the opportunity to succeed and to live securely and well. In this formulation, Belmonte takes the side of the oppressed and, to this extent, can be said to be their advocate. Belmonte in his Marxist class analysis is drawing on the formulations of the materialist theoretical school of political economy, which was at its peak during the second half of the 1970s. At the same time, Belmonte set an example for later postmodern formulations, which, also drawing at least partly on the Marxist tradition, took up advocacy for the oppressed as a central goal of research, replacing discovery and the formulation of general knowledge.

Postmodernism thus combines **relativist epistemology** with **advocacy**. Relativist epistemology emphasizes that all knowledge is influenced by the culture and the social position of the observer, and therefore is subjective, and rejects naturalist claims of scientific objectivity and of the efficacy of rigorous methodologies. Advocacy takes a moral and political position in support of oppressed and subaltern people and peoples—commonly cited are women, people of color, the poor, the workers, under-proletarians, countries of the south, and disadvantaged cultural minorities—and sees as the objective of anthropological accounts the aiding and assisting of such groups. Relativist epistemology and moral advocacy do fit together, for if (as postmodernists argue) objective knowledge is impossible, and thus the discovery of new facts and the formulation of general scientific knowledge are false goals, then the only remaining application of stories about people and their culture and society is moral, as a way of advocating the good against the bad, as a way of advancing the interests of the oppressed and of undermining the oppressors.

THE POSTMODERN WAVE

Postmodern theory crystalized in anthropology in the mid-1980s with, among other works by Clifford and Marcus (1986) and Clifford (1988), *Anthropology as Cultural Critique*, subtitled *An Experimental Moment in the Human Sciences*, by George Marcus and Michael Fischer (1986). The authors draw on influential nonanthropological works on postmodernism, such as Jean-Francois Lyotard's *The Postmodern Condition: A Report on Knowledge* ([1979] 1984), on Geertz's interpretive anthropology, and on Marxist political economy, to formulate a new, postmodern paradigm for anthropology, a paradigm based on subjectivist epistemology and moral advocacy (or, as Marcus and Fischer prefer, "**cultural critique**"). Several innovative elements became prominent in postmodern formulations.

One is the "**problem of representation**," glossed by Marcus and Fischer (1986:86) as a "problem of . . . textual construction" about what should be said about the people and situation studied. But the issue is really about authority, the authority to describe culture, society, and people's lives. In the scientific or realist model, with the researcher striving to be an objective observer, the people of a society and culture were objects to be precisely perceived and recorded. In the postmodern understanding, the researcher is a subjective participant in the life of a society and culture, and the basis of ethnographic knowledge is the dialogue (Jackson 1989:3; Marcus 1994 and passim) between the researcher and the people of the society in which the research is being carried out. This being the case, the people of that society and culture, the people with whom the researcher interacts and shares, must be recognized not as objects, but as subjects in their own rights, as actors with their own agency, and as aware observers of the scene.

If everyone is a subject, who then has the authority to speak about a culture and society, about people and their lives? Is it the researcher, a visiting stranger? Or is it the people themselves who have the authority to speak of their lives? This is the problem of representation. The postmodern answer to the problem of representation is that it is only the people themselves who have the authority to speak about their lives. In this view, ethnographic research must abandon the pretense of observation and reporting in favor of providing local people the opportunity to tell their own stories, that is, in favor of giving voice to local people. The ethnographer—through lecturing, publications, and films—is then able to convey the authoritative voice of local people to a wider audience.

Second, a related problem is how, following this new, postmodern vision, anthropological **texts** should be constructed. The old, **realist** abstract, distanced, impersonal presentation of ethnographic "facts" is seen to be fraudulent, a baseless pretense of objectivity and an illegitimate appropriation of authority. In its place, new literary forms manifesting postmodern sensitivities have to be constructed. One new form of ethnographic report is the more personal accounts, such as those of Briggs and Belmonte, putting the anthropologist in center stage, and conveying the feelings and reactions of the researcher as well as those of the researcher's informants and collaborators from the society. A second variety of ethnographic report takes a more literal **dialogic** form, presenting actual interview protocols that record, word for word, the dialogues between researcher and informants (e.g., Crapanzano 1980; Lavie 1990). Marcus (1994:49) believes that this dialogic form of report relieves the anthropologist from imposing a conceptual framework on the report because "the frame of analysis arises from the voices party to the dialogue." A third way of conceiving an ethnographic report in accord with postmodern sensibilities is labeled "**radical empiricism**" by Jackson (1989:4 and passim).

> A radically empirical method *includes* the experience of the observer and defines the experimental field as one of interactions and intersubjectivity. Accordingly, we make ourselves experimental subjects and treat our experiences as primary data.

Further, "the radical empiricist tries to avoid fixed viewpoints by dispersing authorship, working through all five senses, and reflecting inwardly as well as observing outwardly" (Jackson 1989:8). The ethnographic report thus becomes more phenomenological, experiential, inclusive, inchoate, and by being so is more authentic, genuine, and real (Jackson 1989:16):

> By broadening its empirical field to include participatory knowledge and subjective concerns, anthropology places the knower within the world of the known and gives incompleteness and precariousness the same footing as the finished and fixed. In other words, it urges us not to subjugate lived experience to the tyranny of reason or the consolation of order but to cultivate that quality which Keats called negative capability, the capability of "being in uncertainties, Mysteries, doubts, without any irritable reaching after fact & reason . . ."

Radical empiricism is radical because it roots out the established conceptual, theoretical, and stylistic conventions that we impose on reality as it is experienced, and replaces it with the buzzing, blooming confusion of life.

A third issue is that the part of the anthropologist in research has to be not only acknowledged and recorded, but also self-conscious and reflective, that is, **reflexive**. The reason is that what the anthropologist brings to the research and to the field influences the findings, the results of the research. As one of the early postmodern theorists, Scholte (1969:438–39) puts it,

> The ethnographic situation is defined not only by the native society in question but also by the ethnological tradition "in the head" of the ethnographer. The latter's presuppositions are operative even before entering the field. Once he [or she] is actually in the field, the natives' presuppositions also become operative, and the entire situation turns into complex intercultural mediation and a dynamic interpersonal experience. . . . Since these factors in turn presuppose a pre-understanding (*Vorverständnis*) on the part of both natives and anthropologists, cultural context and personal circumstances precede ethnographic description as such and affect the empirical data gathered.

A much discussed example (see, among others, Jackson 1989:4–5) of reflexive anthropology is Rosaldo's ([1989] 2000) "Grief and a Headhunter's Rage." In this ethnographic and personal account, Rosaldo explains that he could not understand the motivation for or explanations of headhunting among Ilongot of the Philippines, for he ([1989] 2000:523) could not emotionally grasp the connection between grief and rage. "My life experience had not as yet provided the means to imagine the rage that can come with devastating loss." When during fieldwork Rosaldo's wife, the anthropologist Michelle Rosaldo, fell from a mountain path and died of her injuries, Rosaldo ([1989] 2000:522) experienced the rage of grief and finally understood what his Ilongot headhunters had been telling him.

Only after being **repositioned** through a devastating loss of my
own could I better grasp that Ilongot older men mean precisely
what they say when they describe the anger in bereavement as the
source of their desire to cut off human heads. (boldface added)

Reflexivity thus shows that understanding is a function not only of cognitive processes, but of personal experience and position.

The epistemological grounding of research in the researcher's position and experience cannot be avoided, and requires a new kind of reflection and disclosure (Scholte 1969:441; see also Marcus 1994:45): What is
necessary is that "every procedural step in the constitution of anthropological knowledge is accompanied by radical reflection and epistemological
exposition." This epistemological and methodological reflexivity is deemed
necessary for both the producer and receiver of anthropological knowledge, for the producer must assess his or her own findings in terms of the
processes that generated them, and the receiver of the ethnographic information can evaluate those findings only by knowing how they were produced. In practice, this means that ethnographers must disclose in detail
at the very least their social, cultural, and intellectual positions, as well as
the methods by which the information presented was gained. Receivers of
ethnographic information are then, as it is argued, able to assess the likely
shortcomings, gaps, and distortions in the ethnographic report.

Fourth and finally, if the purpose of anthropology is not, and cannot be for epistemological reasons, to build "a natural science of society
and culture" or to discover "the laws of social life," what is its purpose?
What is the point of "a self-reflexive and critical anthropology" (Scholte
1969:448)? The goal of a postmodern anthropology is "firmly based on
the concrete realization of a dialectical and emancipatory praxis . . . in
the . . . context of a radical and political emancipation of concrete
humanity." Or, to put it more prosaically, to improve people's lives.

This orientation, anthropology as moral engagement, is rooted in
the Marxist tradition and its American representatives in the anthropology of the 1960s and 1970s, and, more latterly, feminist anthropology. ". . . [C]ultural relativism, read as moral relativism, is no longer
appropriate to the world in which we live and . . . anthropology, if it is
to be worth anything at all, must be ethically grounded . . ." says
Scheper-Hughes (1995:410), one of the more outspoken and articulate
advocates of committed anthropology. Drawing on her own research in
South American shanty towns and in South Africa, she (1995:411), sees
"little virtue to false neutrality in the face of the broad political and
moral drama of life and death, good and evil, that [are] played out in
the everyday lives [of the marginalized and disadvantaged]." We can no
longer allow our academic preoccupations, she (1995:416) argues, to

> blind us to the banal materiality of human suffering and prevent us
> from developing a political discourse on those hungry populations
> of the Third World that generously provide us with our livelihoods.

"Why," she (1995:416) asks, "do anthropologists so steadfastly refuse to stare back at [evil], to speak truth to its power?"

What, then, is to be done? Scheper-Hughes (1995:415) urges "a radical self-critique" as "a necessary condition for recasting anthropology as a tool for human liberation. . . ." She (1995:419) advocates "an ethnography that is personally engaged and politically committed."

> The new cadres of "barefoot anthropologists" that I envision must become alarmists and shock troopers—the producers of politically complicated and morally demanding texts and images capable of sinking through the layers of acceptance, complicity, and bad faith that allow the suffering and the deaths to continue without even the pained cry of . . . *"The horror! The horror!"* (Scheper-Hughes 1995:417)

Anthropologists, in this vision, must become committed, engaged, morally indignant on behalf of the weak and oppressed, ethically insistent, and politically active. Anthropology should be, first and foremost, a tool for human liberation.

Postmodernism's emphasis on subjectivity, dialogue, reflexivity, and moral commitment is a major departure from the scientific paradigm that dominated anthropology during much of its history. In its wide-ranging theoretical frame, postmodernism comfortably and happily accommodates phenomenological epistemology, Marxist and postcolonial analysis, and feminism.

Chapter Eight

Reflections on Anthropological Theory

In the preceding chapters, I have presented the approaches of anthropological theorists—functionalists, processualists, materialists, symbolicists and structuralists, evolutionists, and feminists and postmodernists—in their own terms, through both illustrations and applications, and by means of their words and my summaries. Further comment has been kept to a minimum.

But the presentation of theoretical views is only part of the story. Equally important are the responses of other anthropologists: the reactions and refinements, debates and disputes, the critiques and rebuttals. Much of the liveliness of theoretical discussion comes from these confrontations. More important, the competition of theoretical ideas in the arena of open debate is the process by which ideas are refined, sharpened, and developed. It is also one of the processes by which theoretical ideas, which for the moment are ascendant or established, are eventually rejected and overthrown.

So there is movement in anthropology as theoretical ideas popular at one time are replaced by other theories, and these new theories are challenged and pushed aside by yet other theoretical formulations. And yet, many diverse theoretical approaches continue to live alongside one another in anthropology. Anthropology is, as Prime Minister Harold Wilson of Great Britain once said about the British Labour Party, a broad church. That is, anthropology has the room and the tolerance to accommodate many different perspectives. Let a thousand flowers bloom!

One reason that many theoretical perspectives continue to be current in anthropology is that anthropologists have long lives. After graduate studies, where theoretical views are likely to be rooted, those anthropologists who take teaching jobs will be active in education and research for some thirty or forty years. Many theoretical perspectives may arise and fall in thirty years, while many anthropologists continue working with the perspective with which they feel comfortable and which they believe valuable and fruitful.

An ongoing part of anthropology is thus the debate that enriches our theoretical discussions and formulations. I would like to provide, next, the briefest of introductions to some of this debate. It is not my intention here to advocate one or another of these arguments or theoretical positions. Rather, this summary of some of the arguments put forth is meant to alert the reader to critical stances taken in the anthropological literature and to some of the specific reasons that some commentators disagree with particular theoretical positions.

CONTRA FUNCTIONALISM

Functionalist approaches, which had held sway in Britain for some thirty years, came under attack at midcentury from a variety of different directions. Perhaps the most serious criticism is that functionalism could not account for the social and cultural change that was so pervasive during that period, especially in the African and Asian colonies in which much British anthropological research had been carried out. A limitation of synchronic studies focusing on life at one moment of time was that the institutions and practices present appeared to be unchanging and inevitable (Harris 1968:516, 526). As has been mentioned, Evans-Pritchard himself criticized social anthropology for not being sufficiently historical, a lack that he tried to rectify in his own work, for example, *The Sanusi of Cyrenaica* (1949) and *The Azande* (1971).

A second criticism is that the explanatory power of functionalism was weak (Harris 1968:529–38). To say that ancestor worship contributes to lineage solidarity does not explain the presence of ancestor worship. The assumption that functional "needs" always generate the means to fill them is called the **functionalist fallacy**. If needs were always filled, every young girl would be a princess and every teenage boy would have a harem. And I would be driving a Jaguar. Even beyond this point, and assuming that what was being explained was lineage solidarity and not ancestor worship, it is not so easy to demonstrate that it was ancestor worship, rather than something else, that led to lineage solidarity. If a society or institution exists, it is easy enough to say that a constituent part contributes to its survival, but is this not more of a circular argument than a powerful explanation?

A third major criticism, this time by cultural analysts (for the latest version, see Sahlins 1999a, 1999b), is that treating cultural beliefs, practices, and institutions in terms of their functions or consequences is reductionistic. That is, directing attention only to the function of an institution ignores the substance of the institution and all of its meaning. The substance of the concepts, ideas, symbols, customs, and practices is lost in functional analysis, and so too are the uniqueness and creativity of cultures. According to this argument, functionalism is not the study of culture, it is anticultural analysis.

A fourth major criticism, by processualists (e.g., Barth 1966), is that functionalism reifies institutions and cultural practices. That is, social and cultural patterns are treated by functionalists as objects and are attributed power to do things, and human individuals are treated as pawns, shunted this way and that by institutions. The reality, according to the processualists, is that only people can be actors, and that so-called institutions and customs are epiphenomena of aggregates of individual choices and behaviors. Once the focus is shifted from institutions to individuals and their choices, social and cultural change loses its mystery, because change results from shifts in individual choices in response to opportunities or constraints.

A fifth criticism of functionalism by structuralists (Lévi-Strauss 1963, 1966) is that it is superficial, raking the surface in search of gold that can only be found by deep mining. The institutions and customs that functionalists examined must be understood not in terms of customs and their functions, but in terms of the basic, underlying principles of organization, the conceptual deep structure, upon which the cultural institutions are based.

CONTRA PROCESSUALISM

Processualism's emphasis on individuals and their choices did not sit well with commentators from various perspectives. For Marxists (e.g., Asad 1973), processualism neglected the different structural positions that individuals were in. As power went along with class position, the criticism went, people's choices and thus their destinies were determined by their structural position. Furthermore, the emphasis on transactions and interest in entrepreneurs was interpreted by some analysts as a kind of monetary reductionism, and processualism was deemed a theoretical apology for (nasty) capitalism.

Structuralists (e.g., Galaty 1980, personal communication) had little regard for the processualist argument that social and cultural patterns were determined by aggregates of individual decisions, for this position neglected the underlying deep cultural structure that provided the reference points and cognitive guidelines for individual decisions. For this reason, processualism appears superficial to structuralists.

For their part, symbolicists (Kapferer 1976) regarded transactionalism and its emphasis on exchange maximization for benefit, like functionalism, as reductionistic. This is because value is established by meaning, and the meanings themselves are subject to negotiation. Thus exchange is above all symbolic, and status or material transfer can take place only within that symbolic framework.

CONTRA MATERIALISM

Materialism argues that, ultimately, ideas are no more than reflections of the material conditions of life. Symbolicists counter that people's lives are culturally constructed by shared meanings, and so too are economy, ecology, and demography. Materialists may say, "given the economy, ecology, and demography," we can tell you what the politics and ideology are going to be. But the economy, ecology, and demography are not "given" in any material sense; they are culturally constructed with concepts and ideas, rules and norms. Knowledge and technology, and morality and medicine, are, first of all, ideas, and these ideas make up the foundations of economy, ecology, and demography. Furthermore, even with information about the culturally based economy, ecology, and demography, there is no way for the materialist to know the cultural substance of politics, religion, and art in any but the most reductionistic and generalizing, trivial and demeaning sense. For example, students of Hinduism and Indian culture were appalled at the crude and superficial treatment of sacred cattle and related ideas by Harris in his materialist account. Finally, political economists and **world system** theorists such as Wolf are criticized for universally applying their own **"master discourse"** to the lives and histories of others rather than listening to the accounts that people and peoples provide for their own lives and experiences.

For processualists and transactionalists, materialism steals away the agency from individual people and posits determination of individuals in general characteristics of the economy and ecology. People are mistakenly treated as puppets by materialists, whereas processualists recognize that people are constantly making choices that form, maintain, and can transform their society and culture.

Materialists, according to postmodernists, hold to an extreme form of positivism, which pretends to view to world objectively and to discover laws of social life, when in reality the materialists are seeing the world and its peoples though their own cultural lens. Furthermore, everyone, including anthropologists, is positioned in social and power structures, and so can see only from that vantage point. So while the positivist (who is usually male) denies his own subjectivity and falsely claims objectivity, he also treats the people he studies as objects, denying them their subjecthood and humanity. Materialists, the argument continues, want to impose their explanations on people, whereas post-modernists encourage the people they study to express their own voice, and, if they are victims of oppression, give them their support.

There is also serious disagreement among materialists themselves. For example, Harris (1979:ch. 6) criticizes the dialectical part of Marxist dialectical materialism as being metaphysical mystification, unscientific, and without any merit. Some other Marxists, such as Jonathan Friedman (1974), view Harris's cultural materialism as "vulgar materialism," simplistic in its view of causality and crude in its view of human life.

CONTRA CULTURE PATTERNS

Anthropologists for whom the discovery of explanation of social and cultural patterns is a central part of anthropology, which would include functionalists (although no one these days would call themselves that), processualists, materialists, and evolutionists, look with dismay at the privileging of meaning in symbolic and structural anthropology, which they deem wholly descriptive and entirely lacking in explanatory power. The surrender of explanation, as they see it, for explication alone, reduces anthropology to ethnography, and a science of humanity to a humanities of symbols. Furthermore, without the test of effective explanation, which could discipline with prediction and retrodiction, each descriptive account must stand only as an interpretation, with no criteria available for judging a good interpretation from a poor one.

For materialists (e.g., Harris 1979:ch. 7 and 9), symbolicists and structuralists wrongly stand Marx on his head by presenting meaning, rather than nature, as the foundation of society and culture. This idealist conception of human life advocated by symbolic and structural anthropology is, however, never put to the test, because no power of explanation is claimed. The basic importance of meaning is asserted but never demonstrated in any fashion. Furthermore, when structuralist formulae—for example, that cannibals boil people of their own societies but roast foreigners—are put to the empirical test by others, they prove to be incorrect (Harris 1979:188–90).

Processualists (e.g., Barth 1994; Vayda 1994) object also to the single patterns identified by symbolic and structural culture analysts, on the grounds that these single patterns simplistically reduce a complex and variable human reality. Vayda (1994:320) devotes his discussion to "the emergence of the view that patterns and order have been exaggerated or unduly emphasized and that variations and variability need to be studied more." He discusses various ethnographies, pointing to the way "the discounting of variations does evince an essentialist bias, involving a quest for 'congruence' and 'unitary symbolic structuring' in . . . symbols and behavior relating to such matters as gender, the landscape, and passage through the life cycle." The culture analysts' focus on a unitary cultural pattern is, from the point of view of processualists, a denial of the individual agency reflected in a variety of different choices and trajectories of action. That each society might contain a number of different and even conflicting cultural patterns, and thus be characterized by a degree of cultural multiplicity (Salzman 1978) rather than uniformity, appears to have been ruled out a priori by the symbolicists and structuralists.

Postmodernists (e.g., Jackson 1989) too reject symbolism and structuralism for its essentialism, abstraction, and overgeneralizing. Cultural analysts strive to find an essential quality, characteristic, or framework from which all or all that is really important in a culture flows, but this, in the postmodern view, is neglecting people and their complex lives in favor of simplistic abstractions. Instead of giving voice to individual people in the culture to tell their own stories, which is the strategy and ethic favored by postmodernists as a solution to the problem of representation, cultural analysts foist their interpretations on a culture, in a kind of culture-analyst imperialism (e.g., the critique of Geertz by Crapanzano [1986] 2000). As well, the simplistic overgeneralizations of the symbolicists and structuralists are particularly in error, according to postmodern commentators, in neglecting people's different placements within the social, economic, and power structures, and the different perspectives that they accordingly have. For postmodernists, there is not one story to be told about a culture, but many stories from different people in different positions. A particular concern for feminist anthropologists is whether "the culture" of a particular society described by symbolicist ethnographers is really men's culture, with women's views and understandings left out. Finally, symbolism and structuralism, following a kind of interested but neutral observer policy, ignores the moral commitment necessary to the neglected, the oppressed, and the subaltern among those whom we study.

Among the symbolic analysts themselves, symbolicists and structuralists are at odds on theoretical issues. For structuralists (e.g., Lévi-Strauss 1963, 1966), the symbolicists' focus on publicly held meanings is superficial, a misdirected emphasis on diffuse manifestations seen in casual chat and occasional winks, rather than on the underlying symbolic foundation of the deep structure. Symbolicists (e.g., Geertz 1973:ch. 13), for their part, see structuralism as forcibly reducing all meaning to sets of simple oppositions and their mediators, a kind of formalist abstractionism gone mad, with deep structures floating somewhere in the universe, exactly where no one is quite sure.

CONTRA EVOLUTIONISM

The nineteenth-century evolutionists were successfully attacked from different perspectives. One critique was from the **diffusionists**, who argued that most societies did not change by invention and innovation, but by borrowing from other societies. Therefore, the argument went, what formed most societies, and what we must examine to understand a culture, is who it was borrowing from and what it borrowed. The diffusionists, like the evolutionists, were mainly armchair anthropologists drawing on the information provided by others to put together a worldwide picture. Some diffusionists took their argument to its (il)logical extreme by asserting that culture was invented in one place, Egypt, and all other cultures were a consequence of diffusion from Egypt.

Both the early evolutionists and the diffusionists were open to the same charges from early fieldworkers, such as the founder of American anthropology, Franz Boas ([1920] 2000), and the founders of British social anthropology, A. R. Radcliffe-Brown and Bronislaw Malinowski. This criticism was that the evolutionists and diffusionists, rather than looking at a society and culture as an organic whole in which the parts were integrated, and in which particular customs and traits gained their meaning and their significance from their place in the whole, an approach labeled **holism**, plucked a ritual from one society, a kinship rule from another culture, and a cultivating technique from a third, in order to drop them into preordained and arbitrary evolutionary or diffusionary categories and schemes.

A further serious criticism (Radcliffe-Brown 1952) was that the historical accounts of the evolutionists (and diffusionists as well) were not based on solid evidence, but were conjectural rather than substantiated. In other words, in the absence of documentary and other evidence—and for many of the African, Asian, and Pacific cultures there was little or no documentary or archaeological evidence—evolutionists and diffusionists were just making up stories about how the past might have been, and calling these stories "history."

Functionalists also took the view that, whatever the state of the historical record, social structure and cultural institutions, and belief and practices, could be best understood in terms of the part they played in contemporary life, rather than in terms of their origins. The functionalist position was that, whatever the origin of customs, their meaning and significance at any particular time arose from their contemporary role in the culture as a whole and in their present interdependencies with other cultural practices. Whatever the origins, the current import of a practice lay in its part in current life. For this reason, explaining cultural features as survivals from an earlier time was a

poor strategy, for it led one away from examining the current and ongoing functions of the belief, rule, or practice.

For materialists (e.g., Harris 1968:ch. 7), the early evolutionists,
Marx and Engels excepted, were not sufficiently materialist, relying on
idealist explanations for evolution. For cultural analysts, evolutionists
submerge cultural diversity in developmental stages, thus reducing the
incredibly rich cultural variation to a few, hierarchically placed categories. For processualists, evolutionary schemes focus on the results of
human activity but ignore the individual agency and choices that generated those results. For postmodernists, evolutionism is one variety of
objectivist positivism and in error on that account. As well, the very
concept of evolution implies or asserts a cultural superiority and inferiority that violates human equality and cultural equivalence. In the
postmodern view, any assertion of superiority and inferiority is ethnocentric, for the judgment of superiority and inferiority is a value judgment, and can come only from one's own culture. The postmodernist
position asserts radical cultural relativism, and any denial of relativism is regarded as an example of cultural imperialism, the imposition
of values from one culture onto another, and is probably racist as well.

Evolutionary ecology has come under severe criticism from materialists, postmodernists, and cultural analysts alike (e.g., Harris 1979:
ch. 5; Sahlins 1976) for reducing culture to biology and for alleged pro-
pensities for racist analysis. There have been suggestions that evolutionary ecology is a latter-day form of **social Darwinism**, a right wing
political philosophy that tries to justify inequality, hierarchy, and even
violence in terms of "survival of the fittest."

CONTRA FEMINISM

There has been little direct criticism in anthropology of feminism
in general, itself a remarkable (and political) fact. However, as we have
already seen, feminist anthropologists differ amongst themselves on
theoretical issues, some drawing on materialism, some on agency, some
on evolution, some on culture theory, and so on, which leads to disagreements. For example, feminist materialists argue that feminist
culture theorists do not give adequate attention to economic class both
within and between societies.

One general criticism of feminist thought as political ideology,
brought from within as well as from external critics of empirical bent,
is that feminism begins not with a set of questions to be investigated,
but with a set of doctrinaire answers that are held on faith and imposed
on ethnographic cases that serve as illustration. Thus, the argument
goes, feminist research cannot learn anything about the world because

it already knows everything from first principles (a criticism leveled also at Marxist anthropology). As a consequence, complex reality is made to fit a simplistic doctrine and theoretical ideas are not tested in a tough-minded fashion.

CONTRA POSTMODERNISM

For anthropologists seeking to explain societal institutions and cultural practices, the postmodern rejection of positive knowledge in favor of subjectivity is abandoning the central quest of anthropology. While postmodernists are correct in arguing that people are subjective and see things from their particular position in the world, they are absolutely incorrect in believing that positivistic science assumes human objectivity. Nothing could be farther from the truth. The scientific method, the heart of science, was invented because it was understood that human error, wish-fulfillment, duplicity, dishonesty, and weakness would commonly distort research findings. The scientific requirements that the procedures of all studies must be specified in detail so that others could repeat them, and the actual replication of findings by other scientists in other venues, were established to minimize the distorting effects of human subjectivity and moral weakness in the quest for knowledge. Science, these critics argue, may not be a good way to understand the world; it is just better than all the rest. The postmodernist wallowing in subjectivity appears, to scientifically minded anthropologists, to be advocating a kind of weak-willed self-indulgence. Instead of doing the hard work of trying to find out about a society and culture by examining it closely, systematically, and judiciously, postmodernists prefer to tell about their own personal experiences in the field, thus becoming the stars of their own ethnographies. Don't we owe more, the critics ask, to the tax-payers who fund our research, the people who give their time and cooperation to provide us information, and the audience (captive, in the case of classes) than self-righteous moralizing and subjectivist posturing? Furthermore, the very epistemological relativism that denies truth in favor of personal and cultural perspectives, is itself logically self-contradictory. It says "every understanding is culturally relative—except this one"; in other words, it asserts that "relativism is absolute." Can a serious discipline be built on such a logical error?

A further criticism is that the claim of the postcolonialist stream of postmodernism, that anthropology is the study of "the other" and its "orientalist" project a demeaning of "the other" in order to enhance our own culture ego, is factually mistaken on both counts. Social and cultural anthropologists have always regarded all societies and cultures, including our own, our neighbors, and our cultural cousins, as well as cultures distant from our own, as subjects for investigation, analysis, and explanation. Furthermore, social and cultural anthropologists have always taken it as their task to seek the logic, reason, and beauty in the cultures they study; as the old definitional joke puts it, "anthropologists are people who apologize for other people's cultures." If anything, anthropologists have been too easy on the people they study, too willing to see virtue and too unwilling to report the negative.

In place of positive knowledge, postmodernism elects moralism as its main mission. The postmodern argument is that, if all understanding is subjective, all knowledge reflects a particular point of view, and thus a particular politics. Because it is impossible to choose between different understandings on the basis of objective truth, the only basis for choosing is political, that is, whose side you want to be on. You can write or accept either a feminist account or a patriarchal account, a postcolonial account or a colonialist account, a prosubaltern account or a hierarchical oppressor account, a proworker account or a procapitalist account. To the critics of postmodernism, the noble anthropological quest of understanding society and culture has been turned into a form of agit-prop (agitation-propaganda) for various ideological crusades. There can be no discoveries, because all answers about society and culture are built a priori into the ideologies imposed on the ethnographic venue studied. In postmodernism, moralizing has replaced understanding, and sloganeering has replaced explanation. According to Marshall Sahlins (1999b:v),

> The problem with such an anthropology of advocacy is not simply that arguments get judged by their morality, but that as a priori persuasive, morality gets to be the argument. The true and the good become one. . . . [And] the moral value is usually an external attribute supplied by (and for) the analyst, . . .

> It is as if other peoples had constructed their lives for our purposes, in answer to racism, sexism, imperialism and the other evils of Western society.

> [This] can amount to using other societies as an alibi for redressing what has been troubling us lately.

Culture analysts have a further objection. The overriding obsession of postmodernism (and its materialist, political economy, and world systems ancestors) with alleged oppressors and supposed victims reduces all human and cultural practice to exploitation, on the one hand, and resistance, on the other. The great range of cultural variation and broad diversity of social organization disappear into these simplistic categories. The structuralist Marshall Sahlins (1999b:v–vi) puts it this way:

What is not too enlightening [about postmodernist analyses] is the way that New Guinea pig feasting, Maori land claims, Zimbabwe medium cults, Brazilian workers' do-it-yourself-housing, Fijian exchange customs, and any number of determinate cultural forms are accounted for, to the [postmodern] anthropologist's satisfaction, by their moral-political implications. It is enough [as far as postmodernists are concerned] to show they [customs] are the effects of or reactions to imperialist domination, as if their supposed hegemonic or counterhegemonic functions could specify their cultural contents. An acid bath of instrumentality, the procedure dissolves worlds of cultural diversity into the one indeterminate meaning. It is something like . . . an intellectual purge of the culture forms, marked by an inflexible refusal to differentiate. It consists of taking the actual cultural content for the mere appearance of a more profound and generic function—in this case, the political or power—and having thus dissolved the historically substantional [sic] in the instrumentally universal, we are pleased to believe we have reduced appearance to truth. . . . So nowadays [under postmodern influences] all culture is [deemed] power. It used to be that everything maintained the social solidarity. Then for a while everything was economic or adaptively advantageous. We seem to be on a great spiritual quest for the purposes of culture things. Or perhaps it is that those who do not know their own functionalism are condemned to repeat it.

Postmodernism, from the cultural perspective, reduces the complex cultural realities of people's lives to the simplistic categories of our own moralizing.

From a neo-evolutionary perspective, postmodernist views seem to neglect historical reality. The postmodernist assertion that all cultures are equal flies in the face of the actual processes of decision making and influence. According to Ernest Gellner (1988:200),

Scientific/industrial civilization clearly is unique, if only in the number of [people] it allows to subsist on Earth, and also because it is, without any shadow of doubt, conquering, absorbing all the other cultures of this Earth. It does so because all those outside it are eager to emulate it, and if they are not, which rarely happens, their consequent weakness allows them to be easily overrun. The prevalent eagerness in turn is so strong just because the new order plainly "works," i.e. it is the key to a technology which confers unparalleled economic and military power, incomparably greater than that ever granted to other civilizations, other visions.

In other words, not withstanding some abstract argument that each culture is, in its own terms, as good as any other, people choose to adopt cultural items, features, and patterns if they seem better. For example, in 1968 when I first began research in Iranian Baluchistan, the nomadic Baluch traveled and transported their goods on camels and used a camel idiom in paying bride price (Salzman 2000b). By my final trip there, in 1976, they were traveling around the desert on large, Russian, two-cycle, gray motorcycle taxis; were sending and receiving goods by pickup truck; and were migrating to and from their date groves in large, open-backed, Mercedes Benz dump trucks. Today among other desert peoples, flocks are now transported from one region to another by truck, and tanker trucks bring water to quench the thirst of the animals (Chatty 1986). So the camels have been phased out, along with the elaborate culture of raising camels, classifying camels, and racing camels. I thought the camels and the culture of raising and using camels were very cool. But the Baluch and other desert dwellers thought that pickups, motorcycles, and heavy trucks were even cooler. Any postmodernist lecturing the Baluch or Bedouin about how camels are as good as motor vehicles would get laughed out of the desert.

A final criticism of postmodernism is the apparently opportunistic adherence to relativism. The postmodern view seems to be that no one has a right to criticize another culture, unless there is something done in that culture that we do not like! A well-known example is the feminist denunciation of gender rules and roles—in, for example, the Mediterranean, Africa, India, East Asia, all Muslim countries, and so forth, in total about 80 percent of humanity, not to mention all societies in human history until 1960—that do not conform to our Western idea of gender equality. Muslim women may claim that they have taken the veil voluntarily as an act of faith, but Western feminists know that this is just **false consciousness**, that these women have been brainwashed to take on the ideas of the patriarchy, and that the veil is a manifestation of the oppression of these women. So the postmodern position seems to be: I stand for human rights; you are ethnocentric; he is racist. If postmodernists do not like what is done in some culture, they are humanitarian; if someone else does not like what is done in some other culture, they are cultural imperialists. Some critics wonder if there is a postmodern double standard.

ASSESSING THEORIES

This sample of theoretical debate sets out some of the arguments between holders of explanatory, explicatory, and advocatory views, between supporters of cultural analysis, materialism, processualism, and so forth, and also within each theoretical approach, between symbolicists and structuralists, dialectical materialists and cultural materialists, and so on. As is obvious, anthropological theories are a matter of open debate, and these debates can lead to refinement and change in theoretical positions, making for a lively disciplinary discourse. Sometimes, however, theories are not challenged and refined but left behind and abandoned in favor of new and novel theories aimed in quite different directions. In these cases, we might wish to ask whether something valuable has been lost.

After this lengthy recitation of criticisms to each of the theoretical points of view, we may wonder how to draw conclusions about the various theoretical positions. But are the debates alone sufficient information from which to draw conclusions? It is important to remember that these heuristic theories are only part of anthropology. Heuristic theories are rather like the introductory sections to cookbooks, "about beef stews" or "about vegetable soups." They guide us with information about what is important, about what we should be looking for. (Marvin Harris [1979:ch. 1]) calls his heuristic theory, cultural materialism, a "research strategy.")

Within the general guidelines provided by these cookbook commentaries, specific recipes are developed. The equivalent in anthropology to these recipes is the substantive theories that indicate the conditions under which we would find general patterns, for example, "nomadic hunters are egalitarian and lacking in distinctions in rank," or that two particular factors are related, for example, "accusations of witchcraft follow lines of repressed conflict." The next step for the cook is to prepare a dish based upon the recipe. For the anthropologist, the parallel step is the ethnographic case study, in the light of the heuristic and substantive theories, of particular people living their lives. Just as the main test of a cookbook commentary and recipe is the tasting of the dish prepared with them, so too the main test of theoretical formulations is in the ethnographic study.

The theories are tested in two senses. One is that the orientations of the heuristic theory and the assertions of the substantive theory are tested by the ethnographic "facts," which can contradict them, for example, if the ethnographer finds that the nomadic hunters she or he is studying do make distinctions of rank among themselves. This is a test of whether the theories are true, or correct. The other kind of test of the theories is whether they lead the ethnographer to construct a rich, informative, rewarding ethnography. And whether the heuristic theory inspires interesting substantive theories. In other words, are the theories fruitful?

Of course, there are other criteria for assessing theories. One is scope. Is the theory comprehensive, covering a wide range of the phenomena in the field, in our case social and cultural life? A second criterion is logical coherence, the degree to which the various parts of the theory fit together. A third criterion is applicability, the extent to which it is possible and practical to define the elements in such a way that it is clear exactly what kind of information is needed to assess the theory. This has been called operational criteria. Can the terms of the theory

be defined in terms of operations of observation or measurement, so
that the theory can be related to specific instances or case studies in
the world?

THE DEVELOPMENT OF THEORIES

Because our subject is theories, I have begun speaking of assessment starting with heuristic theories, and then going down the ladder
of abstraction to substantive theories, and then to particular instances,
ethnographic case studies. But I do not want to give the impression
that anthropological thinking always begins with abstract general theories and then works, deductively, down to individual cases. Nothing
could be farther from the truth. The commonest pattern of anthropological thought is a repeated movement, a kind of constant commuting,
back and forth, up and down, between ethnographic particulars and
theoretical generalities. Perhaps more than in most fields of research,
anthropologists often find their inspiration in their descriptive, ethnographic studies and make inferences from them to a more general, theoretical formulation. The interplay between particular ethnographic
cases and general theories is probably the most fruitful intellectual
process in anthropology, enriching both ethnography and theory.

The generation of theories is not, however, entirely driven solely
by intellectual interests. There are many influences in the origins and
shaping of anthropological theories.

One such influence is the social background of the theorist. For
example, Franz Boas was by origin from a German Jewish family. His
status as a member of a despised minority in Europe led him to oppose
racism by arguing that culture rather than biology (and biological
"race") determines human behavior.

A second type of influence is social developments in the larger
society. For example, the economic and social transformation of western Europe during the industrial revolution led people to believe in
progress. Marxist theory became influential in Europe as a result of the
importance of socialists and communists in European politics. Marxist
theory was constrained in North America by anticommunist sentiments and forces, and became important in North American anthropology after, and to some degree due to, the Vietnam war.

A third type of influence is the intellectual developments in the
wider culture. This can be seen in examples already mentioned. The
rise of racial theories of human behavior in the nineteenth century led
to Boas's rebuttal, and the Enlightenment stimulated theories of evolution. Marxist theory in European social science was available as a
resource for its latter-day arrival in North America.

A fourth type of influence is the interests of a particular segment in society. Anthropological theories of gender and feminist theory developed when large numbers of women became students of anthropology and anthropologists. Here too we can see the influence of wider intellectual trends in the society, for the initiation of these theories came at the same time as the "women's movement" of the 1960s and 1970s, and also social developments, for the women's movement developed in response to changes in women's role as a result of urbanization, declining child rearing, the mechanization of household work, increasing education, and an expanding economy. The recent arrival of "queer theory" in anthropology is a result of the mobilization of homosexual anthropologists.

A fifth type of influence is professional: the social structure of mobility in academic life. While the small scale and hierarchical organization of academic anthropology in Britain led to long-term theoretical continuity, the larger scale and more democratic and segmentary organization of American academia led to greater competition and theoretical innovation. The increasing scale of academic anthropology in America also meant that ethnographies tended to be read by regional specialists, so theoretical works more easily provide broader attention, recognition, and professional rewards. People wrote theory because they found it good to eat.

THE DANGER OF PRESENTISM

> All these people doing what they did beautifully, fully. And I was with them. I wasn't measuring myself against them. What they did before me buoyed me up in the ocean of a shared labor in which we separated by [time], yet breast to breast, dove, were overwhelmed, clung to the sides of a boat and had our hands beaten by oarsmen, and then, sometimes, occasionally, confidently, swam.
>
> —Mary Gordon, *Spending*, p. 87

Anthropologists who would vehemently reject evolutionism and would label the idea of progress as ethnocentric, merrily assert that the newest theory in anthropology is better than anything that came before and reflects a higher state of consciousness and morality. The privileging of the current and demeaning of the slightly less current, not to mention the past, is a presentism that reflects a naiveté and lack of perspective on the history of ideas. Also present is an unattractive inability to extend our much verbalized relativity to the ideas of our colleagues, past and present.

Theoretical presentism feeds into and reinforces various distortions in discussion. The belief that only today's theory has any virtue leads many students to neglect to read past theory, being satisfied with second- or third-hand accounts or evaluations. Just the other day a graduate student said to me that Malinowski could hardly be an authority on methodology, because he spent most of his time avoiding the "natives." When I inquired which of Malinowski's works she had read, she admitted that she had not read any of his books, but she was still sure she knew about Malinowski. Another graduate student repeated a secondhand judgment that Barth's theory was a capitalist theory about profits, and required a close reading of Barth to get beyond the glib labels to the more subtle substance. Presentism leads to simplistic labeling of theories, exaggerating the flaws and ignoring the subtleties of previous theories, and even demonizing of theorists or categories of theorists as capitalists, imperialists, and/or patriarchal oppressors. This treatment of our colleagues, and especially our predecessors, upon whose shoulders we stand, raises serious doubts about our intellectual integrity and our capability to do justice in the study of culture and society.

The importance of recent and past theorists, and the error of presentism, is illustrated by the repeated, fruitful return to their work. It is not uncommon for current theorists to be recycling past work, but with an appropriate makeover, such as new labels. For example, a much lauded paper of Sherry Ortner (1984), which proposed the label "agency" as the new focus for the 1980s' anthropology, was heavily based on the work of the transactionalists of the 1960s, which she duly cited. The old wine is not so bad, but needs a new label. And Ortner was right, there is a great deal of value in the accumulated theory and theoretical debates in anthropology, if we can be open-minded enough to see it.

Glossary

Academic theory (cp. **Folk theory**). A theory held by some members of academic establishments.

Acephalous. Without a head; headless. A term used to characterize social units, such as segmentary tribes, lacking institutionalized leadership roles.

Advocacy. Speaking up and or acting on behalf of a cause of some type; in anthropology, usually on behalf of a person, group, or category of people.

Agency. Action on the part of an individual to advance a goal.

Animism. A type of religious belief in which parts of the natural world, such as animals, plants, winds, and geographical features have spirits that direct their effect on people.

Assumptions. Unproven understandings on which other ideas and knowledge are based.

Bands. Small groups, with population commonly less than one hundred, living partly or wholly autonomously; common among people living by hunting and gathering.

Behavioral. Activity involving the movement of the body.

Behavioral ecology (see **Evolutionary ecology, Sociobiology**). A Darwinian approach to the study of society and culture. Another label for "sociobiology" and "evolutionary ecology."

Binary concepts. A set of opposite concepts, such as cold/hot, in/out, and culture/nature.

Capitalist mode of production. Market-oriented production in which ownership is separated from labor and in which profits are tracked in relation to investment.

Castes, caste system (see **Jati**). A form of organization characteristic of Hindu South Asia in which closed, endogamous groups are identified with certain occupations and are ranked according to the ritual purity or impurity of the occupation.

Catastrophist (cp. **Uniformitarianism**). Someone who holds the belief that changes in the earth and its inhabitants have resulted from extraordinary events, catastrophes.

Chiefdom. A wholly or partly autonomous political entity, commonly with a population numbering in the thousands or tens of thousands, led by a leader without bureaucratic or coercive agencies to support him, who commonly collects and redistributes some economic goods.

Cognition. Thought processes.

Comparative. See **Comparative analysis.**

Comparative analysis. Juxtaposition of cases for examination of commonalities and differences.

Concomitant variation. The relationship between factors or variables that are interrelated and that vary together.

Configuration. Pattern. A cultural configuration is a general cultural pattern into which all of the customs and institutions are woven.

Configurationism. The view that each culture has a dominant pattern into which all cultural elements are woven. An approach favored by Ruth Benedict and, although he does not use this term, Clifford Geertz.

Conscience collective (cp. **Culture**). French phrase used by Emile Durkheim for the beliefs and sentiments held generally by members of a society.

Controlled experimentation. The active attempt to hold constant all potentially influencing factors other than the specific ones being examined. A basic element of scientific methodology.

Correlated (see **Concomitant variation**). Two factors vary together.

Co-vary (see **Concomitant variation**). Short verbal form of "concomitant variation."

Cross-cutting. "Cross-cutting social ties," exist when people united on one basis, for example, residential community, are divided on another basis, for example, descent group membership. A concept developed by Max Gluckman.

Cultural critique. The use of anthropological knowledge to assess and judge cultures, often one's own, for example, as to whether people are free, creative, equal, productive, humane, environmentally sensitive, and so forth. A philosophical and political rather than scientific enterprise.

Cultural idiom. The terms and phraseology in which relationships or other things are conceived and expressed in particular cultures. For example, social relations can be formulated in diverse idioms of·kinship, race, territoriality, class, or political allegiance, among others.

Cultural materialism (see **Infrastructure, Structure,** and **Superstructure**). Materialism is a theoretical approach emphasizing the physical basis of human life and the determining nature of economics. Marvin Harris's version adds ecology and demography as determining factors and stresses the influence of behavior over ideas.

Cultural relativism. The idea that each culture must be understood in its own terms and also that each culture must be judged in its own terms.

Cultural selection. The borrowing by a culture of elements consistent with its basic pattern. An idea of configurationalism.

Cultural system (cp. **Culture**). A definition of culture as the system of symbols and the repository of meaning in a society. A formulation originated by Talcott Parsons and made influential by Clifford Geertz.

Culture (cp. **Cultural system**). Most broadly, everything learned as a member of society.

Darwinian fitness. The ability to produce children for the next generation.

Deconstructing. See **deconstruction.**

Deconstruction. Picking apart a text to find unstated assumptions and implicit values.

Deep structure (see **Binary concepts**). The most basic conceptual framework upon which a culture is based.

Descriptive account (or **Description**). Report of what is observed.

Descriptive generalization (cp. **Theoretical generalization**). Formulation stating the common features of a large class including many examples.

Devolution. Decline from a superior form to an inferior form.

Diachronic. Through time, as in historical studies over a particular time period.

Dialectic. The interaction between two factors and the consequent result. Formulated by Hegel as "thesis," "antithesis," "synthesis."

Dialogic (see **Dialogue**). Of the nature of a dialogue. An argument that ethnographic research is not so much objective observation as it is a dialogue between the researcher and "native" informants.

Dialogue (see **Dialogic**). The conversation between two people.

Diffusion. Borrowing of elements between cultures.

Diffusionism (see **Diffusion**). An approach emphasizing borrowing between cultures for historical understanding. Often seen to be at odds with evolutionism.

Diffusionists. Those holding the view of **diffusionism.**

Emic (cp. **Etic**). For Marvin Harris, the insider's point of view and understanding, seen as being subjective and culture bound.

Empiricism. An epistemological position that knowledge comes from sense data.

Epistemological relativism. The philosophical position that no specific form of knowledge is authoritative, that each culture and subculture has its own form of valid information, and that therefore there may be many culturally defined "truths" but no universal "Truth."

Epistemology, epistemological theory. The study of the sources of knowledge. Various theories—empiricism, rationalism, solipsism—about the sources of knowledge.

Ethnographic field research (see **Participant observation**). Research on a society and culture through residence and direct face-to-face engagement with the people being studied at a site where they are living and in the course of their everyday life. Sometimes called participant observation.

Ethnography. The study of individual societies and cultures. A fundamental part of the anthropologist's work. Also, an account of a particular society and culture. "An ethnography" is the report of the findings of ethnographic research.

Ethnology. The European term for social and cultural anthropology and the comparative study of cultures. For some authors, ethnology implies a historical dimension.

Etic (cp. **Emic**). According to Marvin Harris, the outside observer's point of view, thought to be objective.

Evidence. Information that bears on some question or hypothesis and makes a contribution toward answering or evaluating it.

Evolution. Development from one form to another. Often thought to involve change from lower to higher form, or progress.

Evolutionary ecologists. Those holding to **evolutionary ecology**.

Evolutionary ecology (see **Sociobiology, Behavioral ecology**). An approach that applies Darwinian ideas to the explanation of social and cultural matters.

Evolutionism (see **Evolution**). A theory of development—in anthropology social and cultural development—emphasizing progressive changes from lower to higher forms through internal processes of change and/or stages of development.

Exogamy. Marriage exclusively outside the group.

Explanation (cp. **Explication**). A formulation that accounts for particular cases by showing that they are examples of a general theory or law. An objective of science.

Explication (cp. **Explanation**). A formulation that explores particular cases by delving into their internal structure, meaning, significance, similarity and difference from other cases, and context. A way of understanding characteristic of the humanities.

Facts. Specific descriptive information about particular instances or cases.

False consciousness. Beliefs and understandings about one's position in society that obscure the realities of one's position and one's real interests. An important concept in Marxist theory.

Folk theory (cp. **Academic theory**). The general explanatory beliefs held by people in general in particular societies.

Forces of production. The material assets and conditions making production possible. Along with "relations of production," part of the "infrastructure." Part of Marxist materialism.

Function. The effect that a cultural practice has on another cultural practice.

Functional interrelations. The interconnection and mutual dependence between customs or institutions.

Functionalism. An approach emphasizing the study of the interrelations of cultural elements and the effects of each on every other and the whole.

Functionalist. Someone holding the view of **functionalism**.

Functionalist fallacy. The argument that a cultural practice exists because of the function it provides.

Gemeinschaft. German for "community," implying a small, face-to-face group of people tied to one another for the long term. A concept emphasized by Ferdinand Tönnies.

General evolution (cp. **Specific evolution**). The development of society and culture overall.

Generative models. Substantive theories that explain "social forms" by specifying the processes that generate them. An objective of Fredrik Barth's processual theory.

Gesellschaft. German for "society," indicating a large, impersonal population related by brief and superficial ties. A concept emphasized by Ferdinand Tönnies.

Heuristic theory. A very general, abstract, and not highly precise idea about how the world works. Guides thought and sets an agenda of consideration and investigation.

Historical analysis. The examination of ethnographic cases in terms of their development over time, rather than only at a moment in time. Also the comparison of different periods in a society's history.

Holism. An approach emphasizing the unity of culture and the necessity of understanding any cultural element within its broader context.

Idiographic. Individual, unique, as in accounts of particular cases such as persons, institutions, societies, or cultures. Ethnography, the study of particular societies and cultures, aims for an idiographic account.

Infrastructural determinism. The argument that the infrastructure determines the nature of the "structure" and "superstructure."

Infrastructure (cp. **Structure, Superstructure, Forces of production**). The parts of society and culture directly involved in production. A central concept of Marxist theory.

Institution. An organized pattern of roles, statuses, beliefs, and activities that accomplishes basic tasks in a particular society.

Interdependence. A relationship such that activity or changes in one element has a significant effect in the other.

Interests. The spheres or areas in which people seek or desire benefits, or are thought by others to need benefits.

Interpretation. The formation and inevitable transformation of information as it is processed in a person's perception, cognition, and reporting.

Jati (see **Caste system**). An endogamous kin group that is the basic unit of the caste system.

Kin-ordered mode of production (see **Production, Kinship**). Relations of production are ordered by a kinship idiom. One of Eric Wolf's categories.

Kinship. In anthropology, a type of symbolic idiom, referring to biological ties, that people use to organize themselves. Different forms of kinship organization reflect different versions of the kinship idiom.

Life cycle rituals. Ceremonies to mark culturally determined stages—such as birth, adulthood, marriage, parenthood, death—in human life development.

Lineage (see **Kinship**). A group based on common descent through either the male or female line.

Master discourse. An explanatory framework applied to all cases, such as a social theory applied to all societies irrespective of the views, theories, and explanations held by members of those societies.

Material basis (see **Infrastructure** and **Infrastructural determinism**). Reference to an assumed "infrastructural determinism."

Material relations. Social relations involved directly with production.

Matrilineality. Descent exclusively through the female line.

Mechanical solidarity (cp. **Organic solidarity**). Unity based on similarity and commonality. A concept of Emile Durkheim's.

Mental (cp. **Behavioral**). Having to do with thoughts alone. Important designation in thinking of Marvin Harris.

Meta-theory. Theory about theory. Often a philosophical and epistemological consideration.

Methodological strategy (see **Methodology**). A particular method or set of methods emphasized in a particular discipline or approach.

Methodology. The way in which one goes about collecting information.

Modes of production. Different forms of production, relying on different relations of production, in different societies and historical periods. A concept central to Marxist theory.

Multilinear evolution. The process whereby societies (or other units) develop along different paths with different trajectories.

Naturalism. An epistemological position that as part of nature we can perceive and understand the reality of nature and the nature of reality.

Natural selection. The favoring by natural conditions of some individuals over others in successful reproduction. A basic idea in Darwinian evolutionary theory.

Network. A type of social relations constructed out of dyadic ties, between a number of sets made up of two individuals.

Nomothetic. General, as in general statements or propositions, such as theoretical generalizations about all particular cases within a specific class.

Normative rules. Rules about what is right and wrong.

Objectivity (cp. **Subjectivity**). Perceiving the external object without interference from the observer's sentiments or understandings.

Organic solidarity (cp. **Mechanical solidarity**). Unity based on interdependence resulting from specialization. A concept of Emile Durkheim.

Paradigm. The set of underlying assumptions at the base of an understanding of the world.

Participant observation. The foundation methodology of modern ethnographic research, in which the researcher lives in a setting for an appreciable amount of time, getting to know the people and their activities, and observing them as they go about their lives.

Patrilineality. Descent exclusively through the male line.

Perception, perceptions. The senses that make possible observation, and the observations.

Personality and culture. The study of the interconnection between personality patterns and culture, as well as the position that personality patterns are critical elements in what happens in society.

Philosophy, philosophical (see **Meta-theory**). Considerations and investigations through thought that cannot be resolved through observation.

Political economy. A Marxist theoretical approach emphasizing regional and intersocietal economic and political relations.

Position. Where one fits in the structure of social life.

Positivism. An epistemological position that aims at objective and general knowledge. Consistent with a scientific approach.

Postmodern anthropology (see **Postmodernism**).

Postmodernism. An approach that emphasizes cultural and positional relativity and the inevitable subjectivity that follows. *(Crit Theory)*

Pragmatic. Effective in achieving a goal.

Predict. Assertion that if certain specified conditions hold, another condition will result.

Prestate societies. Decentralized societies, such as bands and tribes, without strong central institutions that monopolize the means of coercion.

Prizes. Whatever is valued by people and leads them to compete with one another. A term used by Frederick Bailey.

Problem of representation (see **Representation**). The postmodern question of who has the right to describe a people and culture, and under what circumstances such a description could be considered legitimate, not to say authoritative.

Process. Sequences of activities in the course of social life.

Processual theory. Approaches that emphasize process as the generator of organization, structure, ideas, values, and rules.

Production. The transformation of raw materials into things or products that can be used by people.

Progress. The idea or fact of improvement, especially in human life, social conditions, and cultural achievement. An important concept in nineteenth-century and some twentieth-century evolutionary theory.

Proven. From a scientific point of view, nothing can be proven in a final and closed fashion, as more information or a new way of looking at things can always change our understandings.

Radical empiricism. Recording what has been seen or heard, with minimal imposition of preconceived ideas and concepts by the researcher. A label used by Michael Jackson for his form of postmodern anthropology.

Rationalism. The epistemological position that knowledge is attained by thought.

Rationality. The application in society, and especially economy, to rigorous standards and precise measurements to judge the attainment of goals.

Realist (and **Realism**). The epistemological position that our observations allow us to perceive reality.

Reciprocal altruism (see **Evolutionary ecology, Darwinian fitness**). Cooperation among kinsmen leading to increased Darwinian fitness for all concerned.

Redistributive economy. Goods are taken up by some central authority and then passed back to people, not necessarily the ones from whom the goods were gotten.

Reflexive (and **Reflexivity**). Self-awareness and critical consciousness in the course of research. An element in postmodern theory.

Relativist epistemology. A position that what you believe is "knowledge" and "truth" is the result of your social position and cultural background and that for someone with a different social position and cultural background something different and perhaps conflicting will be "true." Thus there is no absolute "truth" and no definite "knowledge" that is not culture bound.

Relativity, relativism (see **Cultural relativism**). The idea that the nature of something depends upon what it is in relation with.

Replication. Repeating of an experiment or test by different people in different places to ensure that results are consistent. A central element in the scientific method.

Repositioned (and **Repositioning**). Movement from one social and experiential position to another, and the change of cognitive and emotive frame resulting. An idea of postmodernism.

Representation (see **The problem of representation**, **Voice**). The description of a people and culture.

Ritual pollution. Being impure for sacred, ritual, and social purposes.

Ritual purity. Lacking in any disqualifying defilement for ritual and social purposes.

Science. An approach to knowledge in which ideas and theories are tested by systematic evidence through the use of vigorous methodology.

Scientific epistemology. The position that a highly rigorous methodology can limit error and can separate sound and substantiated knowledge from unsubstantiated ideas.

Segmentary. Made of a set of like units. Said, for example, of tribes made up of many similar villages or kin groups.

Social control. Measures taken to assure compliance with social rules and norms. Includes positive sanctions, or rewards, such as social status and material benefits, and negative sanctions, or punishments, such as incarceration and corporal or capital punishment.

Social Darwinism. A theoretical approach that explains and justifies inequality, hierarchy, and violence in terms of "the survival of the fittest."

Social forms. Specific patterns of social behavior, such as selective marriage ties, limiting terms of group membership, the manner of decision making. A phrase used by Fredrik Barth in his formulation of "generative models."

Social organization. The patterns of social ties among people, including groups, networks, classes, and castes.

Social process. The interactions that take place among people over time, especially repeated, sequential patterns of interaction.

Social relations of production (see **Material relations**). The relationships that people enter into in the course of production, especially those involving ownership or control of resources, labor, supervision of labor, and allocation of products.

Social status. Standing within the community, especially in a graded hierarchy of higher and lower prestige.

Sociobiology (see **Evolutionary ecology, Behavioral ecology**). An approach that applies Darwinian ideas to the explanation of social and cultural matters.

Specific evolution (cp. **General evolution**). The development through time of particular societies.

State-organized societies. Societies in which there is sufficient centralization, monopoly of the means of coercion, such as weaponry, and authority for the government to dominate other forms of organization.

Strategic (see **Strategic decision**).

Strategic decision (see **Voluntaristic**). Decision aimed toward the achievement of a goal.

Structural functionalist (and **Structural functionalism**). One holding the theoretical approach dominant in British social anthropology during the mid-twentieth century. Emphasized the consequences or function of a custom, practice, or institution, and the interconnections between different customs and institutions.

Structuralist. Theoretical adherent of structuralism, especially of the theoretical "school" of Lévi-Strauss.

Structure. A basic pattern of relations. Functionalists spoke of social structure as the ongoing relations or the relations between groups in a society. Structuralists referred to the underlying conceptual and cognitive framework. Marxists placed structure between the underlying and determining infrastructure, and the dependent, ideological superstructure.

Subjectivity (cp. **Objectivity**). Emphasis on the subject or observer rather than the object or the observed. Emphasized in postmodernism.

Substantive theory (cp. **Heuristic theory**). A somewhat general but fairly precise idea about how some aspect or part of the world works. Can be used as an hypothesis and be tested by descriptive evidence from particular cases.

Superstructure. In Marxist anthropology, the elements of culture—such as art, literature, ritual, and philosophy—that reflect the nature of the determining infrastructure and structure.

Supported. Information and data can support an hypothesis or theory rather than decisively prove it, because further evidence can always change the findings and a new, more comprehensive theoretical formulation might supplant the old.

Synchronic. At a particular moment in time, as in a study of a community at a particular moment (or a brief period) with an emphasis on pattern or structure, rather than change.

System. An entity consisting of a number of interrelated subparts.

Text. A body of written statements.

Theoretical generalizations. General propositions that state the relationship between factors or "variables."

Theory (see also **Academic theory, Folk theory, Substantive theory,** and **Heuristic theory**). A general idea or set of ideas that applies to many particular instances. Different types of theory are meant to direct attention to important aspects, or to explain the nature of particular cases, or to predict the relationships between variables.

Transactional (and **Transaction**). Relating to an exchange between people.

Transactionalism. A social theory emphasizing the importance of transactions in the generation and maintenance of social organization and culture.

Transcultural. Extending or crossing cultural boundaries.

Transformation. Shifts in the relations of basic, deep structural concepts that reflect and account for basic differences between cultures. Important concept in structuralist anthropology.

Tribes. The overarching political unit in segmentary societies.

Tributary mode of production. People are forced through coercion to work or to give up what they produce.

Uniformitarian (and **Uniformitarianism**). Holding the assumption, first put forth in early nineteenth-century geology, that natural processes have worked uniformly throughout time. Contrary to catastrophists and creationists.

Unilinear cultural evolution. The idea that all societies had to evolve along the same path and through the same stages.

Universalistic standards. The disinterested assessment of performance, ruling out considerations of social ties and cultural affinities.

Voice (see **Representation, Problem of representation**). People speaking on their own behalf. The desirability of this has been advocated by postmodernism.

Voluntaristic (see **Strategic decision**). An approach emphasizing the choices that people make and the goal-oriented nature of human action.

World systems theorists (see **Political economy**). Those holding a Marxist theory emphasizing the historic integration of the world and the impact of expanding European political and economic influence and control on other societies and peoples.

Appendix II

Culture Theorists

Bailey, F. G. (1924–) British social anthropologist, student of Max Gluckman at the University of Manchester. Developed processual analysis in the study of politics. Author of *Caste and the Economic Frontier* (1957), *Caste, Tribe, and Nation* (1960), *Politics and Social Change* (1963), *Stratagems and Spoils: A Social Anthropology of Politics* (1969), *Humbuggery and Manipulation: The Art of Leadership* (1988), *The Prevalence of Deceit* (1991), *The Civility of Indifference: On Domesticating Ethnicity* (1996), and *The Need for Enemies: A Bestiary of Political Forms* (1998), among other works.

Barth, Fredrik (1928–) Norwegian anthropologist, trained in anthropology also in the United States and England, based first at the University of Bergen, and then Oslo. Major theorist of processualism and transactionalism. Author of *Political Leadership among the Swat Pathan* (1959), *Nomads of South Persia* ([1961] 1986), *Models of Social Organization* (1966), *Ethnic Groups and Boundaries* ([1969] 1998), *Sohar: Culture and Society in an Omani Town* (1983), *Cosmologies in the Making* (1987), and *Balinese Worlds* (1994).

Benedict, Ruth (1887–1948) Early American anthropologist; student of Franz Boas and colleague and collaborator with Margaret Mead. Author of *Patterns of Culture* (1934), a foundation work in cultural anthropology and configurationalist theory. A founder of the school of "personality and culture," she wrote *The Chrysanthemum and the Sword* (1946).

Boas, Franz (1858–1942) Often described as the founder of modern American anthropology. By origin a German, Jewish geographer. Teacher of Margaret Mead, Ruth Benedict, Alfred Kroeber, and many other important American anthropologists of the first half of the twentieth century.

Durkheim, Emile (1858–1916) Nineteenth-century French social theorist. Founder of sociology and anthropology. Introduced powerful concept of culture, for which he used the term *conscience collective*. Among his major works are *Division of Labor in Society* (1893), *The Rules of Sociological Method* (1895), *Suicide* (1897), *Primitive Classification* (1903), and *The Elementary Forms of Religious Life* (1912).

Evans-Pritchard, Edward Evan (1902–1973) British social anthropologist. Student of Radcliffe-Brown. Professor of Social Anthropology, Oxford Univer-

153

sity. Author of *Witchcraft, Oracles, and Magic among the Azande* (1937), *The Nuer* (1940), *The Sanusi of Cyrenaica* (1948), *Kinship and Marriage among the Nuer* (1951), and *Nuer Religion* (1962).

Geertz, Clifford (1926–) American cultural anthropologist; influential founder and advocate of interpretive anthropology, also known as symbolic or semiotic anthropology. Student of Talcott Parsons. Ultimately professor at the Institute of Advanced Studies, Princeton, New Jersey. Author of *The Religion of Java* (1960), *Peddlers and Princes: Social Change and Modernization in Two Indonesian Towns* (1963), *Agricultural Involution: The Processes of Ecological Change in Indonesia* (1963), *The Social History of an Indonesian Town* (1965), *Islam Observed: Religious Development in Morocco and Indonesia* (1968), *The Interpretation of Cultures* (1973), *Meaning and Order in Moroccan Society* (with H. Geertz and L. Rosen, 1979), *Negara: The Balinese Theatre State in the Nineteenth Century* (1980), *Local Knowledge: Further Essays in Interpretative Anthropology* (1983).

Gluckman, Max (1911–1975) British social anthropologist of mid-twentieth century. By origin a South African. Student of Radcliffe-Brown. Built and headed the highly productive Department of Social Anthropology at Victoria University of Manchester. Engaged in extensive ethnographic research in southern Africa. Emphasized an event-oriented research. Author of *The Judicial Process among the Barotse of Northern Rhodesia* (1955), *Custom and Conflict in Africa* (1959), and *Order and Rebellion in Tribal Africa* (1963).

Harris, Marvin (1929–) American anthropologist active in the second half of the twentieth century. During an influential career at Columbia University, continued at the University of Florida, he advanced the theory of cultural materialism in his teaching and writings, both scholarly and popular, including *The Rise of Anthropological Theory* (1968), *Culture, Man and Nature: Introduction to General Anthropology* (1971), *Cows, Pigs, Wars and Witches: The Riddles of Culture* (1974), *Cannibals and Kings: The Origins of Cultures* (1977), *Cultural Materialism: The Struggle for a Science of Culture* (1979).

Lévi-Strauss, Claude (1908–) French theorist of the second half of the twentieth century. Founder of structuralism and Professor of Social Anthropology at the Collège de France. Author of *The Elementary Structures of Kinship* (1949), *The Savage Mind* (1962), *Structural Anthropology* (1963), *The Raw and the Cooked: Introduction to a Science of Mythology I* (1964), among many other works.

Malinowski, Bronislaw (1884–1942) Founder, along with Radcliffe-Brown, of modern British social anthropology. By origin a Polish natural scientist. Taught at London School of Economics. Working in the Melanesian Trobriand Islands during World War I, he set the modern standard for extensive field research. Author of *The Argonauts of the Western Pacific* ([1922] 1984), *Crime and Custom in Savage Society* (1926), *Sex and Repression in Savage Society* (1927), *The Sexual Life of the Savages in North-Western Melanesia* (1929), *Coral Gardens and their Magic* (1935), and *A Scientific Theory of Culture* (1944).

Marcus, George E. (1943–) Contemporary American anthropologist; major postmodern theorist and influence among anthropologists. Coauthor with **Michael Fischer** of *Anthropology as Cultural Critique* (1986). Coeditor with

James Clifford of *Writing Culture: The Poetics and Politics of Ethnography* (1986). His collected theoretical essays are entitled *Ethnography through Thick and Thin* (1998).

Marx, Karl (1818–1873) Nineteenth-century German social theorist who did most of his writing in England. Combined an evolutionary perspective with economic class analysis and a theory of class conflict. Advocate of workers and a future communist society. Wrote *Manifest der Kommunistischen Partei* (The Communist Manifesto; 1848) and *Das Kapital* (Capital; 1859), among many influential works.

Mead, Margaret (1901–1978) American anthropologist and social commentator of early and mid-twentieth century. Student of Franz Boas. Founder of the school of "personality and culture." Author of *Coming of Age in Samoa* (1928), *Growing Up in New Guinea* (1930), *Sex and Temperament in Three Primitive Societies* (1935), and many other works.

Nadel, Sigfried Friedrich (1903–1954) British social anthropologist. By origin an Austrian psychologist and musician. Student of Malinowski. Advocate of comparative analysis. Author of *A Black Byzantium* (1942), *The Nuba* (1947), *The Foundations of Social Anthropology* (1951), and *A Theory of Social Structure* (1957).

Parsons, Talcott (1902–1979) American sociologist and social theorist of mid-twentieth century. Introduced the thought of Max Weber to the English-speaking world. Developed a Weberian, voluntarist approach emphasizing purposeful "action." Headed Department of Social Relations at Harvard University. Author of *The Structure of Social Action* (1937), *Essays in Sociological Theory* (1949), *The Social System* (1951), *Family, Socialization and Interaction Process* (with Robert F. Bales; 1955), and edited (with Edward Shils) *Toward a General Theory of Action* (1951), among other works.

Radcliffe-Brown, Alfred Reginald (1881–1955) British social anthropologist of early and mid-twentieth century. Founder, along with Malinowski, of modern British social anthropology. Major theorist of functionalism. Taught throughout the British Empire and in America, ultimately at Oxford University. His most influential theoretical writings are collected in *Structure and Function in Primitive Society* (1952).

Sahlins, Marshall (1930–) American anthropologist of the second half of the twentieth century. Student of Leslie White at the University of Michigan. Beginning as an evolutionist, converted to structuralism, for which he became a powerful advocate. Contributed to *Evolution and Culture* (1960) and wrote *Tribesmen* (1968), *Stone Age Economics* (1974), *Culture and Practical Reason* (1976), *Historical Metaphors and Mythical Realities* (1981), *Islands of History* (1985), *Anahulu: The Anthropology of History in the Kingdom of Hawaii* (with P. V. Kirch; 1992), *How "Natives" Think* (1995).

Steward, Julian (1902–1972) American researcher of mid-twentieth century. Student of Alfred Kroeber. Developed a materialist version of ecological theory, presented in his influential *Theory of Culture Change* (1955).

Weber, Max (1864–1920) Nineteenth-century German sociologist and social theorist; founder of sociology and anthropology. Compared societies and civilizations, and examined the evolution of rationality in social organization.

Took a voluntarist view, emphasizing people's purposes and choices. Major works include *The Protestant Ethic and the Spirit of Capitalism* (1904–1905), *The Methodology of the Social Sciences* (essays published originally in 1904–1917), and *The Theory of Social and Economic Organization* (Part I of *Wirtschaft und Gesellschaft*); see also *From Max Weber: Essays in Sociology* (Garth and Mills, eds.).

White, Leslie (1900–1975) American anthropologist of mid-twentieth century. Professor at the University of Michigan. Major twentieth-century evolutionist. His two main works are *The Science of Culture* (1949) and *The Evolution of Culture* (1959).

Wolf, Eric R. (1923–1998) Born in Central Europe; immigrated to the United States just before WWII. Student of Julian Steward. Prominent anthropologist throughout the second half of the twentieth century. A specialist on Latin America with interest in the peasantry and its place in the broader society. Marxist in theoretical approach, he pursued analysis in terms of the broader political-economy. Among his publications are *Sons of the Shaking Earth* (1959), *Peasants* (1966), *Peasant Wars of the Twentieth Century* (1969), *Europe and the People without History* (1982), and *Envisioning Power* (1999).

Further Reading

Anthropological Theories: A Guide Prepared by Students for Students, Department of Anthropology, University of Alabama. http://www.as.ua.edu/ant/faculty/murphy/anthros.htm   A very helpful, detailed Web site account of (so far) 16 "schools" of anthropological theory.

Anthropological Theory: An Introductory History, R. Jon McGee and Richard L. Warms, eds. (Mountain View, CA: Mayfield, 1996). A useful collection of 38 readings, mostly reprinted articles, chapters, or excerpts of major anthropological theorists of the twentieth century. The editors provide brief comments on schools of theory and on individual articles.

Cultural Materialism: The Struggle for a Science of Culture, Marvin Harris (New York: Random House, 1979). Includes a four-chapter presentation of cultural materialism and a seven-chapter review of alternative, mistaken theories. A highly opinionated and tendentious, but thought provoking and amusing, account. (See also *The Rise of Anthropological Theory*).

Culture Theory, David Kaplan and Robert A. Manners (Englewood Cliffs, NJ: Prentice Hall, 1972; reissued Prospect Heights, IL: Waveland Press, 1986). A thoughtful review in 212 pages of issues in anthropological theory during the middle third of the twentieth century.

Encyclopedia of Cultural Anthropology, David Levinson and Melvin Ember, eds. (New York: Henry Holt, 1996). An extremely valuable four-volume work of substantial original articles on all aspects of anthropology, including major theories and theorists. Appendix listing anthropological periodicals.

Encyclopedia of Social and Cultural Anthropology, Alan Barnard and Jonathan Spencer, eds. (London: Routledge, 1996). An excellent 658-page volume of brief, original articles on all aspects of anthropology, including major theories and theorists. Biographical appendix and glossary included.

A History of Anthropological Theory, Paul A. Erickson (Peterborough, Ontario: Broadview Press, 1998). A brief survey of anthropological theory from antiquity to today in 149 pages of text. In addition are appendices of review questions, glossary, and suggested readings.

An Introduction to Theory in Anthropology, Robert Layton (Cambridge: Cambridge University Press, 1997). A review in 241 pages of seven major theoretical schools in recent and contemporary anthropology.

The Rebirth of Anthropological Theory, Stanley R. Barrett (Toronto: University of Toronto Press, 1984). A critical review of issues in anthropological theory.

The Rise of Anthropological Theory: A History of Theories of Culture, Marvin Harris (New York: Thomas Y. Crowell, 1968). A highly opinionated and tendentious, and rewarding, history of theory in 806 lively pages. (See also *Cultural Materialism*.)

Sociocultural Evolution, Bruce G. Trigger (Oxford: Blackwell, 1998). A scholarly review of theories of sociocultural evolution and of criticisms of these theories, from the earliest times to the present.

Theory in Anthropology, Department of Anthropology, Indiana University. http://www.indiana.edu/~wanthro/theory.htm   A student Web site covering anthropological associations and subdisciplines, biographies of some influential theorists, and other useful and informative topics.

Theory in Anthropology: A Sourcebook, Robert A. Manners and David Kaplan, eds. (Chicago: Aldine, 1968). A wide-ranging collection of fifty-three reprinted articles, book chapters, or excerpts that were important contributions to anthropological theory during the middle third of the twentieth century.

References

Asad, Talal. 1973. *Anthropology and the Colonial Encounter*. London: Ithaca Press.

Bailey, F. G. 1957. *Caste and the Economic Frontier: A Village in Highland Orissa*. Manchester: Manchester University Press.

———. 1969. *Stratagems and Spoils: A Social Anthropology of Politics*. Oxford: Basil Blackwell.

Barth, Fredrik. (1961) 1986. *Nomads of South Persia*. Prospect Heights, IL: Waveland Press.

———. 1966. *Models of Social Organization*. Occasion Paper No. 23. London: Royal Anthropological Institute of Great Britain and Ireland.

———. 1994. "A Personal View of Present Tasks and Priorities in Cultural and Social Anthropology." In *Assessing Cultural Anthropology*, ed. R. Borofsky. New York: McGraw-Hill.

Beauchesne, Eric. 23 December 1999. "We're Living Longer, Healthier." *Montreal Gazette*, A8.

Beck, Lois. 1986. *The Qashqa'i of Iran*. New Haven, CT: Yale University Press.

Belmonte, Thomas. 1979. *The Broken Fountain*. New York: Columbia University Press.

Benedict, Ruth. (1935) 1961. *Patterns of Culture*. London: Routledge and Kegan Paul.

Bishop, Charles, and Toby Morantz, eds. 1986. *Who Owns the Beaver? Northern Algonquian Land Tenure Reconsidered*. Special issue of Anthropologica NC 18(1–2).

Blok, Anton. (1974) 1988. *The Mafia of a Sicilian Village, 1860–1960*. Prospect Heights, IL: Waveland Press.

Boas, Franz. 1920. The Methods of Ethnology. *American Anthropologist* 22(4). (Reprinted in *Anthropological Theory: An Introductory History, 2/E*, ed. R. J. McGee and R. L. Warms. Mountain View, CA: Mayfield, 2000.)

Boddy, Janice. 1989. *Wombs and Alien Spirits: Women, Men, and the Zar Cult in Northern Sudan*. Madison: University of Wisconsin Press.

Bossen, Laurel. 1975. "Women in Modernizing Societies." *American Ethnologist* 2(4): 587–601.

Briggs, Jean. 1970. *Never in Anger: Portrait of an Eskimo Family*. Cambridge, MA: Harvard University Press.

Chagnon, Napoleon. 1979. "Is Reproductive Success Equal in Egalitarian Societies?" In *Evolutionary Biology and Human Social Behavior: An Anthropological Perspective*, ed. N. A. Chagnon and W. Irons. North Scituate, MA: Duxbury Press.

Chatty, Dawn. 1986. *From Camel to Truck: The Bedouin in the Modern World*. New York: Vantage.

Clifford, James. 1988. *The Predicament of Culture: Twentieth-Century Ethnography, Literature, and Art*. Cambridge, MA: Duxbury.

Clifford, James, and George E. Marcus, eds. 1986. *Writing Culture: The Poetics and Politics of Ethnography*. Berkeley: University of California Press.

Crapanzano, Vincent. 1980. *Tuhami: Portrait of a Moroccan*. Chicago: University of Chicago Press.

_____. 1986. "Hermes' Dilemma: The Masking of Subversion in Ethnographic Description." In *Writing Cultures: Poetics and Politics of Ethnography*, ed. J. Clifford and G. Marcus. Berkeley: University of California Press. (Reprinted in *Anthropological Theory: An Introductory History, 2/E*, ed. R. J. McGee and R. L. Warms. Mountain View, CA: Mayfield, 2000.)

Cronk, Lee, Napoleon Chagnon, and William Irons, eds. 1999. *Adaptation and Human Behavior*. Hawthorne, NY: Aldine de Gruyter.

Dahrendorf, Ralf. 1968. *Essays in the Theory of Society*. London: Routledge and Kegan Paul.

Delaney, Carol. 1991. *The Seed and the Soil: Gender and Cosmology in Turkish Village Society*. Berkeley: University of California Press.

Durkheim, Emile. (1893) 1933. *The Division of Labor in Society*. Glencoe, IL: Free Press.

Eiseley, Loren. 1959. *Darwin's Century: Evolution and the Men Who Discovered It*. London: Victor Gollancz.

Evans-Pritchard, E. E. 1937. *Witchcraft, Oracles, and Magic among the Azande*. Oxford: Clarendon.

_____. 1940. *The Nuer: A Description of the Modes of Livelihood and Political Institutions of a Nilotic People*. Oxford: Clarendon.

_____. 1949. *The Sanusi of Cyrenaica*. Oxford: Clarendon.

_____. 1951. *Kinship and Marriage among the Nuer*. Oxford: Clarendon.

_____. 1956. *Nuer Religion*. Oxford: Clarendon.

_____. 1962. *Essays in Social Anthropology*. London: Faber and Faber.

_____. 1971. *The Azande: History and Political Institutions*. Oxford: Clarendon.

Fagan, Brian M. 1999. *Archaeology: A Brief Introduction*, 7th ed. Upper Saddle River, NJ: Prentice Hall.

Firth, Raymond. 1964. *Essays on Social Organization and Values*. London: Athlone.

Frank, Andre Gunder. 1966. The Development of Underdevelopment. *Monthly Review* 18:17–31.

Frazer, Sir James George. (1890) 1960. *The Golden Bough: A Study in Magic and Religion*. New York: Macmillan.

Freeman, Derek. 1983. *Margaret Mead and Samoa: The Making and Unmaking of an Anthropological Myth*. Cambridge, MA: Harvard University Press.

Fried, Morton H. 1975. *The Notion of Tribe*. Menlo Park, CA: Cummings.

Friedman, Jonathan. 1974. "Marxism, Structuralism and Vulgar Materialism." *Man* (N.S.) 9:444–69.

Galaty, John G. 1979. "Pollution and Pastoral Antipraxis: The Issue of Maasai Inequality." *American Ethnologist* 6(4): 803–16.

Galaty, John G., and Douglas L. Johnson. 1990. "Introduction: Pastoral Systems in Global Perspective." In *The World of Pastoralism: Herding Systems in Comparative Perspective*, ed. J. G. Galaty and D. L. Johnson. New York: Guilford.

Geertz, Clifford. 1963. *Agricultural Involution: The Processes of Ecological Change in Indonesia*. Berkeley: University of California Press.

_____. 1968. *Islam Observed: Religious Development in Morocco and Indonesia*. New Haven, CT: Yale University Press.

_____.1973. *The Interpretation of Cultures*. New York: Basic Books.

_____.1979. *Meaning and Order in Moroccan Society*. Cambridge: Cambridge University Press.

_____. 1980. *Negara: The Theatre State in Nineteenth-Century Bali*. Princeton, NJ: Princeton University Press.

_____. 1983. *Local Knowledge: Further Essays in Interpretive Anthropology*. New York: Basic Books.

_____. 1988. *Works and Lives: The Anthropologist as Author*. Stanford, CA: Stanford University Press.

Gellner, Ernest. 1988. *Plough, Sword and Book: The Structure of Human History*. Chicago: University of Chicago Press.

George, Shanti. 1990. "Agropastoral Equations in India." In *The World of Pastoralism: Herding Systems in Comparative Perspective*, ed. J. G. Galaty and D. L. Johnson. New York: Guilford.

Gluckman, Max. 1940. "Analysis of a Social Situation in Modern Zululand," *Bantu Studies* XIV.

_____. 1942. "Some Processes of Social Change Illustrated with Zululand Data," *African Studies* I.

_____. 1959. *Custom and Conflict in Africa*. Glencoe, IL: Free Press.

Grant, Nicole J. 1995. "From Margaret Mead's Field Notes: What Counted as 'Sex' in Samoa." *American Anthropologist* 97(4): 678–82.

Greene, John C. (1959) 1996. *The Death of Adam: Evolution and Its Impact on Western Thought*. Ames: Iowa State University Press.

Harris, Marvin. 1966. "The Cultural Ecology of India's Sacred Cattle." *Current Anthropology* 7:51–66.

_____. 1968. *The Rise of Anthropological Theory*. New York: Thomas Y. Crowell.

_____. 1974. *Cows, Pigs, Wars and Witches: The Riddles of Culture*. New York: Random House.

_____. 1977. *Cannibals and Kings: The Origins of Cultures*. New York: Random House.

_____. 1979. *Cultural Materialism: The Struggle for a Science of Culture*. New York: Random House.

_____. 1994. "Cultural Materialism Is Alive and Well and Won't Go Away Until Something Better Comes Along." In *Assessing Cultural Anthropology*, ed. R. Borofsky. New York: McGraw-Hill.

Hawkes, Kristen. 1993. "Why Hunter-Gatherers Work: An Ancient Version of the Problem of Public Goods." *Current Anthropology* 34(4): 341–61.

Hawkes, Kristen, J. F. O'Connell, and N. G. Blurton Jones. 1997. "Hadza Women's Time Allocation, Offspring Provisioning, and the Evolution of Long Postmenopausal Life Spans." *Current Anthropology* 38(4): 551–77.

Hymes, Dell. 1969. *Reinventing Anthropology*. New York: Pantheon.

Irons, William. 1975. *The Yomut Turkmen: A Study of Social Organization among a Central Asian Turkic-Speaking Population*. Anthropological Papers No. 58. Ann Arbor: Museum of Anthropology, University of Michigan.

———. 1979a. "Preface." In *Evolutionary Biology and Human Social Behavior: An Anthropological Perspective*, ed. N. A. Chagnon and W. Irons. North Scituate, MA: Duxbury.

———. 1979b. "Some Statements of Theory." In *Evolutionary Biology and Human Social Behavior: An Anthropological Perspective*, ed. N. A. Chagnon and W. Irons. North Scituate, MA: Duxbury.

———. 1979c. "Cultural and Biological Success." In *Evolutionary Biology and Human Social Behavior: An Anthropological Perspective*, ed. N. A. Chagnon and W. Irons. North Scituate, MA: Duxbury.

———. 1994. "Why Are the Turkmen Not More Stratified?" In *Pastoralists at the Periphery: Herders in a Capitalist World*, ed. C. Chang and H. A. Koster. Tucson: University of Arizona Press.

Jackson, Michael. 1989. *Paths Toward a Clearing: Radical Empiricism and Ethnographic Inquiry*. Bloomington: Indiana University Press.

Kapferer, Bruce, ed. 1976. *Transaction and Meaning: Directions in the Anthropology of Exchange and Symbolic Behavior*. Philadelphia: Institute for the Study of Social Issues.

Kelly, Robert L. 1995. *The Foraging Spectrum*. Washington, DC: Smithsonian Institution Press.

Kroeber, A. L. (1923) 1948. *Anthropology: Race, Language, Culture, Psychology, Prehistory*, rev. ed. New York: Harcourt, Brace.

Kuper, Adam. 1988. *The Invention of Primitive Society*. London: Routledge and Kegan Paul.

Lancaster, William. (1981) 1997. *The Rwala Bedouin Today*. Prospect Heights, IL: Waveland Press.

Lavie, Smadar. 1990. *The Poetics of Military Occupation: Mzeina Allegories of Bedouin Identity under Israeli and Egyptian Rule*. Berkeley: University of California Press.

Leach, Edmund. 1970. *Lévi-Strauss*. London: Fontana/Collins.

Leacock, Eleanor. 1978. "Woman's Status in Egalitarian Societies: Implications for Social Evolution." *Current Anthropology* 19:247–75 (including critical comments by other authors).

———.1983. "Interpreting the Origins of Gender Inequality." *Dialectical Anthropology* 7(4): 263–84. (Reprinted in *Anthropological Theory: An Introductory History, 2/E*, ed. R. J. McGee and R. L. Warms. Mountain View, CA: Mayfield, 2000.)

Lee, Richard B. 1993. *The Dobe Ju/'hoansi*, 2nd ed. Fort Worth, TX: Harcourt, Brace.

Lévi-Strauss, Claude. (1949) 1969. *The Elementary Structures of Kinship (Les structures élémentaires de la parenté)*. London: Eyre and Spottiswoode.

———. (1962) 1966. *The Savage Mind (La pensée sauvage)*. London: Weidenfeld and Nicolson.

———. (1962) 1969. *Totemism (Le Totémisme aujourd'hui)*. Harmondsworth, England: Penguin Books.

———. 1963. *Structural Anthropology*. New York: Basic Books.

_____. (1964) 1969. *The Raw and the Cooked: Introduction to a Science of Mythology: I (Le cru et le cuit: Mythologiques I)*. New York: Harper and Row.

_____. 1966. *Du miel aux cendres: Mythologiques II*. Paris: Plon.

_____. 1968. *L'origine des maniéres de table: Mythologiques III*. Paris: Plon.

Lewis, I. M. 1961. *A Pastoral Democracy: A Study of Pastoralism and Politics among the Northern Somali of the Horn of Africa*. London: Oxford University Press.

Lukes, Steven. 1972. *Emile Durkheim, His Life and Work*. New York: Harper and Row.

Lyotard, Jean-Francois. (1979) 1984. *The Postmodern Condition: A Report on Knowledge*. Minneapolis: University of Minnesota Press.

Malinowski, Bronislaw. (1922) 1984. *Argonauts of the Western Pacific*. Prospect Heights, IL: Waveland Press.

_____. (1925, 1948) 1992. *Magic, Science and Religion and Other Essays*. Prospect Heights, IL: Waveland Press.

_____. (1944) 1960. *A Scientific Theory of Culture*. Chapel Hill: University of North Carolina Press.

Marcus, George E. 1994. "After the Critique of Ethnography: Faith, Hope, and Charity, But the Greatest of These Is Charity." In *Assessing Cultural Anthropology*, ed. R. Borofsky. New York: McGraw-Hill.

Marcus, George E., and Michael M. J. Fischer. 1986. *Anthropology as Cultural Critique: An Experimental Moment in the Human Sciences*. Chicago: University of Chicago Press.

Marwick, M. G. 1965. *Sorcery in Its Social Setting: A Study of the Northern Rhodesian Cewa*. Manchester: Manchester University Press.

Marx, Karl, and Friedrich Engels. 1845–1846. "Feuerbach: Opposition of the Materialist and Idealist Outlook." (Reprinted in *Anthropological Theory: An Introductory History*, ed. R. J. McGee and R. L. Warms. Mountain View, CA: Mayfield, 1996.)

Mead, Margaret. (1928) 1973. *Coming of Age in Samoa*. New York: Morrow Quill.

Morgan, Lewis Henry. 1877. "Ethnical Periods." (Reprinted in *Anthropological Theory: An Introductory History*, ed. R. J. McGee and R. L. Warms. Mountain View, CA: Mayfield, 1996.)

Murdock, George Peter. 1949. *Social Structure*. New York: Macmillan.

Murphy, Robert F., and Julian H. Steward. 1956. "Tappers and Trappers: Parallel Process in Acculturation." *Economic Development and Cultural Change* 4:335–53.

Nadel, S. F. 1951. *The Foundations of Social Anthropology*. Glasgow, Scotland: The University Press.

_____. 1952. "Witchcraft in Four African Societies: An Essay in Comparison." *American Anthropologist* 54(1): 18–29.

Nelson, Ruben F. 1 January 2000. Letter in *National Post*, B9. Toronto: Canada.

Ortner, Sherry. 1974. "Is Female to Male As Nature Is to Culture?" In *Woman, Culture, and Society*, ed. M. Z. Rosaldo and L. Lamphere. Stanford, CA: Stanford University Press.

_____. 1984. "Theory in Anthropology Since the Sixties." *Comparative Studies in Society and History* 26(1): 126–66.

Parsons, Talcott. 1937. *The Structure of Social Action*. New York: Free Press.

_____. 1951. *The Social System*. New York: Free Press.

_____. 1964. *Social Structure and Personality*. New York: Free Press.

Price, Barbara. 1978. "Secondary State Formation: An Explanatory Model." In *Origins of the State: The Anthropology of Political Evolution*, ed. R. Cohen and E. R. Service. Philadelphia: Institute for the Study of Human Issues (ISHI).

Radcliffe-Brown, A. R. 1948. *A Natural Science of Society*. Chicago: University of Chicago Press.

_____. 1952. *Structure and Function in Primitive Society*. London: Cohen and West.

Rogers, Susan Carol. 1975. "Female Forms of Power and the Myth of Male Dominance: A Model of Female/Male Interaction in Peasant Society." *American Ethnologist* 2(4): 727–56.

Rosaldo, Renato. 1989. "Grief and a Headhunter's Rage." (Reprinted in *Anthropological Theory: An Introductory History, 2/E*, ed. R. J. McGee and R. L. Warms. Mountain View, CA: Mayfield, 2000.)

Sahlins, Marshall. 1960. "Evolution: Specific and General." In *Evolution and Culture*, ed. T. G. Harding, D. Kaplan, M. D. Sahlins, and E. R. Service. Ann Arbor: University of Michigan Press.

_____. 1976. *The Use and Abuse of Biology: An Anthropological Critique of Sociobiology*. Ann Arbor: University of Michigan Press.

_____. 1981. *Historical Metaphors and Mythical Realities: Structure in the Early History of the Sandwich Islands Kingdom*. Ann Arbor: University of Michigan Press.

_____. 1999a. "Two or Three Things that I Know about Culture." *Journal of the Royal Anthropological Institute* (N.S.) 5:399–421.

_____. 1999b. "What Is Anthropological Enlightenment?" *Annual Review of Anthropology* 28:i–xxiii.

Salzman, Philip Carl. 1978. "Ideology and Change in Middle East Tribal Societies." *Man* (N.S.) 13:618–37.

_____. 1983. "Why Tribes Have Chiefs: A Case from Baluchistan." In *The Conflict of Tribe and State in Iran and Afghanistan*, ed. Richard Tapper. London: Croom Helm.

_____. 1999. *The Anthropology of Real Life: Events in Human Experience*. Prospect Heights, IL: Waveland Press.

_____. 2000a. "Hierarchical Image and Reality: The Construction of a Tribal Chiefship." *Comparative Studies in Society and History* 42(1): 49–66.

_____. 2000b. *Black Tents of Baluchistan*. Washington, DC: Smithsonian Institution Press.

Schapera, Isaac. (1943) 1970. *Tribal Innovators: Tswana Chiefs and Social Change 1795–1940*. London: Athlone Press.

Scheper-Hughes, Nancy. 1995. "The Primacy of the Ethical: Propositions for a Militant Anthropology." *Current Anthropology* 36(3): 409–20.

Schneider, Jane, and Peter Schneider. 1976. *Culture and Political Economy in Western Sicily*. New York: Academic.

Scholte, Bob. 1969. "Toward a Reflexive and Critical Anthropology." In *Reinventing Anthropology*, ed. Dell Hymes. New York: Pantheon.

Service, Elman R. 1971. *Cultural Evolutionism*. New York: Holt, Rinehart & Winston.

_____. 1975. *Origins of the State and Civilization: The Process of Cultural Evolution*. New York: Norton.

Shankman, Paul. 1996. "The History of Samoan Sexual Conduct and the Mead-Freeman Controversy." *American Anthropologist* 98(3): 555–67.

Slocum, Sally. 1975. "Woman the Gatherer: Male Bias in Anthropology." In *Women in Perspective: A Guide for Cross Cultural Studies*, ed. R. Reiter. New York: Monthly Review Press. (Reprinted in *Anthropological Theory: An Introductory History, 2/E*, ed. R. J. McGee and R. L. Warms. Mountain View, CA: Mayfield, 2000.)

Spear, Thomas, and Richard Waller, eds. 1993. *Being Maasai: Ethnicity and Identity in East Africa*. London: James Curry.

Spencer, Herbert. 1860. "The Social Organism." (Reprinted in *Anthropological Theory: An Introductory History*, ed. R. J. McGee and R. L. Warms. Mountain View, CA: Mayfield, 1996.)

Spiro, Melford. 1979. "Whatever Happened to the Id?" *American Anthropologist* 81(1): 5–13.

Stocking, George W., Jr. 1992. *The Ethnographer' Magic and Other Essays in the History of Anthropology*. Madison: University of Wisconsin Press.

Tönnies, Ferdinand. (1887) 1957. *Community and Society*. New York: Harper and Row.

Trigger, Bruce G. 1998. *Sociocultural Evolution*. Oxford: Blackwell.

Turner, V. W. 1957. *Schism and Continuity in an African Society: A Study of Ndembu Village Life*. Manchester: Manchester University Press.

Tylor, Edward Burnett. 1871. "The Science of Culture." (Reprinted in *Anthropological Theory: An Introductory History*, ed. R. J. McGee and R. L. Warms. Mountain View, CA: Mayfield, 1996.)

Van Kirk, Sylvia. 1987. "Toward a Feminist Perspective in Native History." In *Papers of the Eighteenth Algonquian Conference*. Ottawa: Carleton University.

Vayda, Andrew P. 1994. "Actions, Variations, and Change: The Emerging Anti-Essentialist View in Anthropology." In *Assessing Cultural Anthropology*, ed. R. Borofsky. New York: McGraw-Hill.

Wallerstein, Immanuel. 1974. *The Modern World-System: Capitalist Agriculture and the Origins of the European World-Economy in the Sixteenth Century*. New York: Academic.

Weber, Max. (1904–1905) 1930. *The Protestant Ethic and the Spirit of Capitalism*. London: George Allen and Unwin.

_____. (1925) 1947. *The Theory of Social and Economic Organization*, ed. Talcott Parsons. Glencoe, IL: Free Press.

White, Leslie. 1959. *The Evolution of Culture*. New York: McGraw-Hill.

_____. 1943. "Energy and the Evolution of Culture." (Reprinted in *Anthropological Theory: An Introductory History*, ed. R. J. McGee and R. L. Warms. Mountain View, CA: Mayfield, 1996.)

Williams, Roger L. 1964. *Modern Europe 1660–1945*. New York: St. Martin's Press.

Wolf, Eric R. 1982. *Europe and the People Without History*. Berkeley: University of California Press.

_____. 1994. "Facing Power." In *Assessing Cultural Anthropology*, ed. R. Borofsky. New York: McGraw-Hill.

Index